HOW TO FORM A MICHIGAN LLC* (*LIMITED LIABILITY COMPANY) BEFORE THE INK DRIES!

A Step-by-Step Guide, With Forms

by Phillip G. Williams, Ph.D.

Small Business Limited Liability Company Series
Volume 1

first edition

The P. Gaines Co.

PO Box 2253, Oak Park, Illinois 60303

Library of Congress Cataloging in Publication Data

Williams, Phil, 1946-
    How to form your own Michigan limited liability company before the ink dries! : a step-by-step guide, with forms / by Phillip G. Willams.
    p.   cm. -- (Small business limited liability company series : v. 1)
    Includes index.
    ISBN 0-936284-45-5 (pbk. : alk. paper)
    1. Private companies--Michigan--Popular works.   I. Title.
  II. Series.
  KFM4407.Z9W55   1997
  346.774'0668--dc21   96-48991
                                               CIP

Cover design by BENSEN STUDIOS, Arlington Heights, Illinois

Manufactured in the United States of America

Table of Contents

INTRODUCTION

Contrary to the proverb which says, "There is nothing new under the sun," a completely new way of doing business in the United States has recently emerged. This innovative form of business is called the limited liability company (often referred to, in short, as the LLC).

The existence of this new business entity forces us to rethink our options. Traditionally, persons wishing to start a business had three choices. They could operate as: (1) a sole proprietorship, (2) a partnership, or (3) a corporation. We must now add to this menu a fourth selection, the limited liability company. In Chapter 1, we will see how this new option of the LLC stacks up against the other three in terms of advantages and disadvantages.

Perhaps you are planning to start a business. Or you are already in business, operating as a sole proprietor or a member of a partnership. You want to know if you can benefit from running your business as a corporation or a limited liability company. This book will examine the pros and cons of each, with the focus on the limited liability company. All the forms needed to set up a Michigan limited liability company, as authorized by the Michigan Secretary of State, are included in tear-out form in the back of this book. [1]

First, let us take a moment to consider the roots of this new concept, the limited liability company. The first state to enact LLC legislation was Wyoming. In 1977, a Wyoming law created the first U.S. limited liability company. If this law had passed in a large state like California or New York, it would probably have quickly been duplicated in other states. Five years passed before another state (Florida) passed similar LLC legislation, however. The Internal Revenue Service issued a key ruling in September of 1988 (Ruling 88-76) on the tax treatment of LLCs. This important ruling clarified the tax status of this new type of business entity and opened the floodgates. State after state in rapid succession authorized the LLC as a form of doing business. Today, all 50 states (including Michigan) and the District of Columbia recognize the limited liability company format.

---

1   The P. Gaines Co, also publishes a book specifically for Michigan which highlights the corporate form of organization, walks you through the steps of incorporation, and provides all the needed forms in a tear-out format. The title of that volume is *How to Form Your Own Michigan Corporation Before the Inc. Dries!* To order a copy, call our tollfree number or send in the order form in the back of this book.

A number of businesses can benefit from organizing themselves as a limited liability company. Anything from a small business to a large multinational enterprise can operate effectively as an LLC. Some legal practitioners are now saying that the LLC will quickly become the preferred form of business operation for all companies, except those that are publicly traded on stock exchanges.

Some states allow one individual operating alone to form a limited liability company, but most currently require a minimum of two persons to form an LLC. There is, however, good reason to suppose that this requirement of a minimum of two members will be abolished soon, for reasons that will be examined later in the book. Some states, such as Pennsylvania, are already amending their laws to allow one person to set up an LLC. There are ways around the two-person minimum in Michigan which will also be looked at later.

If you presently have two or more related[2] individuals who are interested in going into business, then the LLC format may be ideally suited to your needs. An association of two or more professional practitioners, such as engineers, dentists, or architects, may also organize themselves as an LLC. There are some very clear-cut advantages for professional associations to organize as an LLC instead of a corporation, which will be discussed in Chapter 6, "The Michigan Professional Limited Liability Company."

The major advantages of operating as an LLC include limited liability, less restrictions on who its members are than is the case with corporate shareholders, much less formality and paperwork than the corporate form of business, greater financial flexibility in divvying up profits or losses among the members, and taxation at individual rather than corporate rates.[3] One disadvantage is the newness of this concept. Consequently, not all of the kinks have been worked out of the laws yet, which may possibly lead to more instability in the legal and tax realms. We will discuss the extent to which changes in the law governing Michigan LLCs may be anticipated and what the nature of these may be.

The present book, designed to clarify the important business area of limited liability company formation, is written specifically for Michigan individuals and businesses, providing a thorough discussion of the advantages and disadvantages of LLCs, tax angles, employee benefits, and a blueprint for setting up your own Michigan LLC. In the back of this book we provide all the forms necessary to organize a Michigan LLC. If you wish to form a Michigan LLC

---

2   By "related" individuals, we mean simply two persons who have joined together as a team, whether they are relatives, spouses, partners, or friends.

3   As noted previously, this book will show a technique whereby one person can set up a limited liability company in Michigan. It is important to realize that the owner of such a one-person LLC can choose to be taxed as either a proprietorship or a corporation on the federal level. Taxwise, one or the other may prove more advantageous, depending on your individual circumstances.

as a team of doctors, veterinarians, dentists, public accountants, psychologists, engineers, architects, or other licensed professionals, you will find this type of LLC explained in Chapter 6.

The remainder of this introduction will focus on the situations in which LLCs are especially recommended and those in which they are not advisable.

When LLCs Work Best

Certain common business situations lend themselves especially well to LLC operation. These include (1) existing partnerships, (2) startup companies, including home-based, (3) women- and minority-owned businesses seeking government contracts, (4) highly profitable existing businesses, (5) small businesses in general desiring a hands-on management style of operation, and (6) someone considering an S corporation.

• In the first case, by switching an existing partnership to an LLC format, you gain the best of both worlds. Your business will still receive pass-through tax treatment so

income is taxed at the individual partners' rates. But the LLC also gives you a liability shield for all the partners—not just the limited partners.

• In the second instance, the owners of a startup company that experiences losses in the early months or years of the business will be able to deduct those losses on their individual tax returns, as a limited liability company. This is an advantage primarily if you have other sources of taxable income. If you draw a salary from other employment, have investment income, or income from another business, the losses from the LLC will reduce dollar for dollar your personal taxable income. In the case of a corporation, present losses are deductible only on the corporate tax return—not on your individual return—on a carry forward basis against future profits, if any, of the corporation.

• In the third instance, women- and minority-owned businesses seeking government contracts, the LLC format is ideal in providing the owners with limited liability. In addition, its gives the business sufficient formal structure and organization to satisfy most government contract requirements without the burdensome details of operating as a corporation.

• In the fourth case, the LLC format also works well with a very profitable enterprise. A profitable corporation with, say, at least half a million dollars in annual income, will likely be hit at some point with the double whammy of two federal taxes— individual and corporate—once the corporation reaches the cap set by the IRS on retained earnings and has to start paying out part of its profits in dividends. The LLC form allows you to escape the entity level tax and pay only the individual owner's tax due on his or her share of profits, thus escaping the double tax.

• In the fifth case, management of a small business organized as an LLC is generally much less formalized than that of a corporation. Small LLCs are commonly managed by the members themselves although larger LLCs may follow the corporate model and hire non-members as professional managers. The smaller, member-managed LLC favors the kind of hands-on management, with collective decision-making, that many small business owners are seeking.

• In the last instance, an LLC and an S corporation have the same legal and tax advantages: both offer limited liability to the owners and pass-through tax treatment. The LLC, however, is not restricted to 35 shareholders,[4] like an S corporation; there is no limit on the number of members it can have; the LLC, furthermore, can have individual members as well as other legal entities, such as partnerships and corporations, as members, unlike the S corporation. The LLC, furthermore, is much simpler to operate. The owners of an S corporation can accidentally forfeit their S status and not even realize it for years. S corporation tax laws are that complex. In the event of such an unintended conversion from S status to regular corporation status,

the owners may be hit with a big, unexpected tax bill years down the road. With the LLC, what you see is what you get. An LLC does not have the power to unexpectedly transform itself, like one of those video game icons that suddenly metamorphoses into a mobile mouth and starts to gobble up everything in its path.

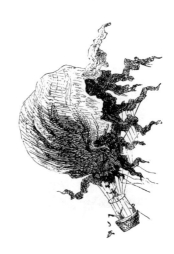

When LLCs May Not Be a Good Idea

By the same token, there are situations in which LLC formation is especially not advised.

• First and foremost is that of an existing corporation. To convert your present corporation to an LLC will usually involve sizeable legal expense and unfavorable tax consequences. If you feel that you must do so anyway, be sure to consult an attorney.

---

4   Traditionally, S corporations have been limited to 35 shareholders. A new law has now raised the number of shareholders allowed S corporations to 75.

• We have also mentioned that LLC statutes in most states, including Michigan, require a minimum of two owners, definitely a drawback for the one-man band contemplating LLC status. Chapter 3 of this book will show you a loophole that will allow you to operate as a one-person LLC in Michigan. The procedure requires a little fancy footwork, but it is not difficult. Under proposed IRS guidelines, the single-owner business operating as an LLC will now have the option of being taxed as a sole proprietor, at his or her individual tax rate, or at corporate rates. Since the top corporate rates are lower than the top individual rates, this may prove to be an advantage unless the business is profitable enough to trigger the infamous corporate "double tax."

To Use a Lawyer or Not to Use a Lawyer—That Is the Question

If you decide to go the LLC route and you prefer to do your own LLC formation without a lawyer, you are entitled to do so, since you are not required by Michigan law to use an attorney to organize your business as an LLC. Since the average attorney fee for this type of business organization can run from the hundreds to the thousands of dollars, you will save money by doing the work yourself. On the other hand, if you already have a prospering business and little time to concern yourself with the details of a business reorganization, you can find a competent attorney skilled in this area through the local chapter of the American Bar Association.

If you do prefer to use the services of an attorney to handle your LLC formation, the information provided herein will help you ask the right questions of your attorney and make the most informed decisions. If you decide to fill out and file your own LLC organization papers, we recommend having an attorney review them, since even simple organizations can have "complications." You will still save money by following this procedure, since the charge for this service at an hourly rate (approximately $100) will be substantially less than the full organization fee.

Even if you decide to organize your LLC without the aid of a lawyer, we strongly advise that you check with a tax adviser to see that the LLC format makes sense for your particular business from a tax viewpoint.

If there are unusual aspects to your LLC formation that are not treated in the following discussion, we also advise legal consultation prior to filing the Articles of Organization.

11

Chapter 1. FOUR FORMS OF BUSINESS OWNERSHIP

Until recently, the federal and state governments of the United States and their agents such as the IRS have recognized three legal forms of business ownership: the sole proprictorship, the partnership, and the corporation. Today, all 50 states (and the District of Columbia) have now adopted yet a fourth form of business operation, called the limited liability company. We will look at the pros and cons of each form of doing business. While this book is primarily concerned with the category of the limited liability company, it is important to examine the other three by way of comparison. Each has distinct advantages and disadvantages.

Sole Proprietorship

If you operate your own business and have not incorporated or entered into a partnership agreement, you are automatically classified as a sole proprietor. In other words, a sole proprietor is one person engaged in a business for profit. The chief advantage of this form of operation is its informality. You can start up or terminate your business whenever you feel like it. The state or federal government cannot prevent you from starting this type of business, so long as it is not illegal (an unauthorized gambling operation or a large distillery in your basement might invite government intervention, for example).

The sole proprietor can also freely mix personal and business finances, lumping all the money into one bank account or handling it however he or she pleases. Of course, the sole proprietor, like all business owners, has to pay taxes, so he must apply for a state sales tax number, keep records, file state and federal tax returns and follow all other procedures required by law. But as the least regulated of the four forms of business ownership, the sole proprietorship does not require permission from the state for its formation, operation, and dissolution.

Furthermore, the sole proprietor may transfer the inventory of his business to personal use. In the case of the corner grocery store, the owner may simply choose to eat what he does not sell. If the store owner wants to take a chicken from his meat case or a cantaloupe from his fruit stand, he is free to do so.[1] If an employee of a corporation followed the same procedure, however, he would be guilty of theft.

The major disadvantage of the sole proprietorship—and this also holds true for partnerships as well—is that the owner is personally liable for all the debts of the business and for any injuries caused to or by its employees acting in a business capacity. If your warehouse clerk drops a 50-gallon drum on his own head or on the head of one of your customers, for example, then you are personally responsible for the damages.[2]

All business entities, whether corporations, limited liability companies, partnerships, or sole proprietors, generally carry insurance, if they can get it. Regardless of whether or not your company can afford insurance, however, both the corporate form and the limited liability company form of doing business *in themselves* offer a valuable protection against unlimited liability. This is clearly not the case with the sole proprietor.

As sole proprietor, not just your business assets are "at risk." If you owe creditors more than your business is worth or if a legal suit against you awards the plaintiff an amount in excess of your business assets, your personal assets as well—your bank account, your car, your home, your Persian rugs—may all be legally attached, and your salary garnisheed if you have other employment as well.[3]

Your liability as a sole proprietor is limited only by the totality of all your possessions, personal as well as business.

The other area in which the sole proprietor is at a distinct disadvantage is that of fringe benefits. C corporations enjoy the most business "perks," sole proprietors the least. C corporations, for example, can deduct the cost of medical insurance they provide to both owner-employees as well as non-owner-employees. Sole proprietors, by contrast, can deduct their employees' medical insurance costs in full but only 30 percent of their own on their personal tax returns. The other 70 percent is deductible as a medical expense only when the proprietor itemizes and medical expenses exceed 7.5 percent of adjusted gross in-

---

1 It should be noted, however, that even the sole proprietor is required, for tax purposes, to keep a record of inventory adopted for personal use. This information is needed in completing the 1040 Schedule C form.

2 Insurance is one means of protection, although it is often an expensive way to limit personal liability. It may also be virtually impossible for the small business person to obtain at affordable rates.

3 Every state has laws which exempt certain personal possessions from attachment to satisfy debts, so a creditor cannot literally take the clothes off your back. Chapter 7 debtors faced with liquidation of their assets have federal exemptions of $15,000 on their home ($30,000 for married couples), $2,400 on their car, and, under federal law, $1,500 on any implements, professional books, or trade tools. Under Michigan law, a specified number of cows, chickens, and other livestock are also covered by this exemption from seizure!

come. C corporations garner a number of other benefits not available to proprietors: group term life insurance up to $50,000 per individual; a $5,000 death benefit; the deduction of medical reimbursements to all employees, including shareholder-employees; loss deductions up to $50,000 per year ($100,000 if filing jointly) under Section 1244 of the Internal Revenue Code; and tax breaks on Social Security and employment taxes.

Realistically speaking, many small businesses have no choice but to start existence as a sole proprietorship if the owner does not have sufficient time and resources to deal with the greater complexity entailed by other forms of business organization. If the enterprise prospers, however, either incorporation or organizing as a limited liability company will become, in time, an increasingly attractive option.

Expert Advice on Sole Proprietorships and Accounting

An excellent book on starting and running a sole proprietorship is Bernard Kamoroff's Small Time Operator: How to Start Your Own Business, Keep Your Books, Pay Your Taxes, and Stay Out of Trouble! *This book also includes a thorough treatment of accounting practices for the small business and contains enough actual ledger sheets and worksheets to last for a full year. This publication can be ordered from The P. Gaines Co. See the order form in the back of this book.*

Partnership

A partnership is a business for profit which is owned by two or more individuals. Partnerships resemble sole proprietorships, with special allowances demanded by the fact of more than one owner. Thus, the same advantages which the sole proprietor enjoys apply to the partnership as well, the lack of formal requirements being the chief benefit. There exist no special procedures for establishing a partnership; a simple verbal agreement is sufficient, although a written agreement in the event of future disagreements among partners is highly advisable.

Termination of the partnership is automatic upon the death, disability, or withdrawal of one of the partners (unless otherwise agreed). Another important advantage of the partnership is that it provides a framework for individuals to pool their resources, including money, skills, and ideas. In a partnership, the sum is often greater than the parts, since it permits persons acting together to achieve goals that none could attain individually.

The federal government's Uniform Partnership Act defines a partnership as "an association of two or more persons as co-owners of a business for profit." This act regulates the activities of partnerships in every state. It stipulates that the partners share equally in the profits and the losses, unless otherwise agreed. In a partnership, each partner owes the partnership a fiduciary duty to put the business interests of the partnership first. If partnership business is being siphoned off by one of the partners for his own use without the knowledge and consent of the other partners, that particular partner is guilty of defrauding the partnership and may be sued by the other principals.

In addition, each partner may enter a business deal that legally binds the partnership, as long as the business falls within the scope of business customarily undertaken by the partnership. Since each partner has full authority to act as the agent of the partnership, a lot is riding on the abilities and scruples (or lack thereof) of your fellow partners under such an agreement.

As in the case of the sole proprietor, the partnership must follow all procedures, keep all records, and remit all forms and payments required by the state and federal taxing authorities. The partnership itself is not a taxable entity, however. The partnership annually reports its income to the IRS on an informational return (Form 1065), and the individual partners include their share of the profits on their personal 1040 tax returns. Thus a partnership determines its income and pays taxes in basically the same way as an individual sole proprietor.

Like the sole proprietor also, the chief disadvantage of the partnership is the personal liability of each partner for the debts of the partnership. All partners in a business are individually liable for all acts of the business. If your partner(s) is (are) unscrupulous or unwise, you stand to lose a great deal more than your initial investment.

In short, the risks of partnerships are extensive, since partners have unlimited liability for all actions or omissions of the partnership or its individual partners, employees, or others acting in its name and behalf.

Another disadvantage: When the assets of the partners are disproportionate and you are the partner with much greater assets, you forfeit more in the event that partnership assets are inadequate to satisfy creditors' claims. In such an eventuality, your house may be attached and liquidated to pay business debts, whereas your undercapitalized partner may lose only her truck! When you consider that a creditor can go after the one partner with the most assets, even though all the partners are responsible for an unpaid debt, you may think twice before entering this kind of relationship. Of course, the partner being pursued by creditors can sue the other partners to try partly to recover his or her disproportionate losses.

In summary, general partnerships are less expensive to start than corporations or LLCs because most states do not require the filing of a form and the payment of a fee to set up a general partnership. If a partnership is set up properly, it will require about the same preparation as a corporation or an LLC: partnerships need to start off with a sold written partnership agreement, just as corporations require bylaws or LLCs need to adopt operating agreements. While general partnerships involve a similar amount of tax form preparation and related paperwork as LLCs, corporations are by far the most complex and time-consuming business entities to administer. The biggest drawback to partnerships is that they do not provide the liability shield that corporations and LLCs offer. Like sole proprietorships, partnerships are also excluded from most of the fringe benefits available to C corporations.

Limited partnership. Finally, under the Uniform Partnership Act there exists a special type of partnership called the "limited partnership," which combines aspects of a partnership and a corporation. A limited partnership has two classes of partners, defined as general and limited partners. The general partners assume the operation of the business. In a regular partnership, discussed above, all the partners are general partners. A limited partner, on the other hand, can invest in a partnership without involvement in its management and without the risk of personal liability. Unlike the general partner who has unlimited personal liability, the liability of the limited partner does not exceed the amount of his initial investment. Unlike a regular partnership, a limited partnership agreement, according to state law, can only be established in writing.

Many types of real estate investment groups, for instance, will have both general partners who organize the venture and limited partners who invest in it. While the limited partner is shielded from liability over and above his original investment, he is not allowed to participate in management of the company. Only a general partner can do that. Interestingly enough, a marriage is considered a general partnership unless there is a written agreement in advance that it is to be treated as a limited partnership!

Corporation

A corporation is a legal entity separate from its owner(s), manager(s), or operator(s). As a "legal person," it can conduct business, borrow and lend money, sue and be sued. Wanda Gold decides to incorporate her business and forms Wanda Gold Enterprises, Inc. Although Wanda is the sole owner and operator, her corporation in the eyes of the state has a distinct life of its own, separate from that of Wanda. It will be expected to pay taxes like a real person, it may enter into contracts, be named as a defendant or plaintiff in a lawsuit, acquire and hold property, and so on.

As already noted, regular (C) corporations provide their shareholder-owners with a liability shield and a number of fringe benefits not available to other business entities.

16

The corporation is the most formal of the four ways of doing business and the most regulated by state and federal laws. Unlike the sole proprietorship and the partnership, a corporation cannot be formed until you receive written approval from the state. The life of a corporation, its "birth," begins with the issuance of the Articles of Incorporation by the Secretary of State and ends with its voluntary or involuntary dissolution (as in the case of bankruptcy). The Michigan corporation statutes define the rules and procedures governing the formation, continuance, and termination of Michigan corporations. For a complete discussion of how to set up a Michigan corporation, with step-by-step instructions and all needed forms in a tear-out format, consult our publication, *How to Form Your Own Michigan Corporation Before the Inc. Dries!* To obtain a copy, see the order form in the back of this book.

S corporation. The S corporation is a special "small business corporation" which traditionally had no more than 35 shareholders. A recently passed law now allows for 75 shareholders in the case of this type of small corporation. The S corporation closely resembles an LLC in many respects. It is taxed like a partnership, with income or losses being passed through to the individual owners. Because of its advantageous tax status, its owners cannot receive the fringe benefits that regular (C) corporation owners are entitled to. The main problem with this type of business entity is its complexity. One may advertently or inadvertently lose one's S status and not even know about it for years, owing to the Byzantine tax regulations governing its for-

mation and operation. In such an eventuality, amended tax returns would have to be filed for the years in question and any additional taxes due paid.

Michigan close corporation. Another alternative is to form a special type of corporation termed a "close corporation." Michigan law, unlike that of many states, requires no special steps to set up this form of business, apart from filing the standard Articles of Incorporation. Therefore, it will involve simply stating in the Articles of Incorporation or the bylaws of the corporation that the corporation will be operated under a shareholders' agreement whereby the shareholders will assume the responsibility of directors in all matters. This one statement, in effect, eliminates a whole layer of corporate management and thereby simplifies the organizational structure of the business considerably. The informality of this type of corporation is its biggest virtue. In this respect, it compares favorably with an LLC. It will still be taxed at corporate rates, unlike an LLC, whose profits are passed through and taxed at the individual owners' personal rates.

Limited Liability Company

The limited liability company is a hybrid form. Combining features of a corporation and a partnership, the LLC allows its owners to enjoy the limited liability of the corporate structure while being taxed like a partnership. Thus, the income or loss of the LLC flows through to the individual

17

owners and appears on their personal income tax returns.

One possible drawback for the individual business owner: in Michigan, the LLC legally requires a minimum *of two* members to set up at present, like a partnership, although there is a way around this rule. It seems likely that all states will eventually allow one-member LLCs, since there is no compelling reason not to do so. (Several states that originally stipulated a minimum of two members for this form of business have gone back and revised the laws to allow single-member LLCs). If you are thinking about going into business but are not yet ready, by the time you get your ducks in line, the law in this area may very well have changed. If you are starting a business as a single individual and are seriously considering the LLC format, also see Chapter 3 for details on a strategy you may use to get around this two-member requirement.

Another drawback: in a two-member LLC, if one member withdraws for any reason, including death, the LLC is automatically dissolved. In such a situation, the remaining member would either have to reorganize the business as a sole proprietorship or a corporation or find another member to continue its existence as an LLC under current Michigan law. The final option is to reorganize as a single-member LLC as explained in Chapter 3.

Another feature of Michigan LLCs: an LLC has to have a limited period of existence in order to receive pass-through tax treatment, although the Michigan law does not specify what that period is. Traditionally, the period of existence of an LLC is 30 years. You will need to specify the period of existence of the LLC in its Articles of Organization (see Appendix A). This is a mere formality and does not require you to dissolve your business on the date specified.

What would be the advantage of forming an LLC instead of a corporation? In some situations, there would be no advantage, since an S corporation would usually, although not always, give you the same tax structure as an LLC: the income or loss from the S corporation is divvied up among the individual owners just like a partnership or an LLC. In one area at present, S corporations are more flexible than LLCs, since one-owner S corporations are allowed and encouraged.. While we have devised a strategy, as already alluded to, for setting up a one-member LLC in Michigan, thus putting S corporations and LLCs on a completely equal footing, to do so does require some additional time and expense.

In other situations, clearcut advantages of LLCs appear: an S corporation is limited to 75 shareholders, whereas an LLC can have an unlimited number of members (in reality, however, most LLCs, if they want to be member-managed, are not going to be able to operate effectively with many more than 35 members). Also, S corporation shareholders must be U.S. citizens or resident aliens; LLCs do not have these limitations and may admit foreign members. In addition, business entities, such as other corporations or partnerships, may be members of an LLC, thus allowing the establishment of various types of joint ventures between individuals and businesses under the LLC framework. This is not allowed with S corporations.

One big advantage of an LLC over an S corporation is its flexibility in income allocation or loss among the members. If you are a 50 percent owner of an S corporation's stock, you would pay 50 percent of the taxes on income. Members of an LLC are not tied to this rigid percentage schedule in dividing up the income or loss. Members holding equal shares of the business may divvy up the profits or losses in different tax years in ways that give them less or more income than their proportional share, thus improving their tax picture.

Setting up and running an LLC involves much less formality and paperwork than that of a corporation. In addition, professional associations reap benefits in several specific areas by organizing as an LLC instead of a corporation: buyouts and pension plans.

One area in which the formation of an LLC proves ideal is that of joint ventures. Say, for instance, that a graphic designer and a printing company want to form a joint venture to sell a line of greeting cards. A partnership is one option but an LLC has the obvious advantage of limiting liability. If the greeting card venture folded and creditors were owed substantial amounts, in the case of a general partnership the creditors could go after the assets of the individual partners. With an LLC, however, this is not the case. The personal assets of each of the members of the LLC would be off limits to creditors seeking to recover debts incurred by the LLC.

LLCs are often recommended for foreign investment, venture capital, joint ventures, real estate, oil and gas and high technology transactions. If you plan to be involved in any ventures of this type, we recommend that you explore the advantages and disadvantages of this type of operation, compared to the corporate form of doing business, with a competent legal adviser.

As noted in the Introduction, the key advantages of LLCs over sole proprietors, partnerships, and corporations, are that they limit your personal liability (which proprietorships and partnerships do not), yet they are much easier to form and operate, with less paperwork, than corporations. Currently, they are taxed on the federal level like partnerships; on the state level, they may be taxed as either corporations or partnerships (the tax situation in Michigan is unusual, in that all business entities, whether sole proprietorships, corporations, partnerships, or LLCs, pay the same amount of tax once they reach a certain size). This means that the income of the LLC will be taxed at the individual rates of the members rather than at corporate rates on the federal level but will be subject to a Michigan state tax, discussed in Chapter 4. Since LLCs are a hybrid form, they combine the best aspects of proprietorships (ease of operation), corporations (limited liability), and partnerships (taxation at individual rates).

Now let's take a closer look at some of the key aspects of the limited liability company as a form of business ownership.

Limited liability

The majority of individuals forming Michigan limited liability companies will enjoy the advantage of limiting personal liability by means of the LLC structure. LLCs, in fact, enjoy the same limitation of personal liability as corporations. Limiting liability is traditionally one of the greatest incentives for organizing your business as an LLC. An LLC member is not, in most cases, personally liable for the debts of the company. Therefore, if a lawsuit is brought against Wanda Gold Enterprises, L.L.C., only the assets of the business itself will be subject to collection, not the personal assets of Wanda herself (with certain important exceptions noted hereafter). This fact can be very comforting to someone just starting out in business.

From the standpoint of limiting liability, the LLC route may be worth it in terms of peace of mind alone. Not only will the members not be liable for the debts of the business, over and above their investment in the company. Risk ventures can also be undertaken with the same assurances— only the investment of the company will be "at risk," not personal property.

In the event of a financial disaster, limited liability companies, like individuals, can go bankrupt. If your company suddenly owes creditors half a million dollars and the assets of the company are only $20 thousand, then the business could file for bankruptcy. Once the $20 thousand in assets was distributed to creditors, the bankruptcy court would declare the business to be legally dissolved and the remainder of the company debt would in effect be wiped out. You would then be free to start another limited liability company tomorrow with a new name, if you so desired.

This is not, of course, a recommendation that you form a limited liability company and amass huge debts and then cancel them out by filing for bankruptcy. Not only would such an intentional attempt to evade payment of bills be unethical, but most creditors would be unwilling to extend a large line of credit to you in the first place unless you were an established customer.

If it were apparent, moreover, that you intentionally formed a "thin" (undercapitalized) limited liability company in order to escape payment of debts, you would in all probability not escape personal liability. The courts in such cases in the past have tended to subject the owners of such businesses to personal liability. The point is that in the event of a major unforeseeable disaster—a lawsuit, large casualty loss, and so on—bankruptcy is a final "escape clause" for LLCs [4] which, unlike the sole proprietorship and the partnership, allows your personal assets to remain untouched.

4 Everything said about limiting liability through the formation of a limited liability company thus far applies to corporations as well. Both the corporation and the limited liability company share this same essential trait of being able to eliminate personal liability of the owners, in most cases.

The cases in which liability is *not* limited by the LLC structure generally fall into one of three categories: (1) taxes; (2) instances of gross negligence, fraud, mismanagement, or malpractice (especially in the case of professional service businesses); (3) personal assets pledged to secure a loan.

Regarding the matter of taxes, remember that the payment of taxes is the lifeblood of the state and federal governments. Strict laws and penalties safeguard this form of governmental livelihood. In this delicate area, even LLCs are not exempt from sanctions, and, in some situations, a member of an LLC can be held personally liable for failure to withhold and pay taxes (if this is one of the defined duties of the member, as treasurer, for instance).

Second, professional malfeasance may also trigger personal liability, as in the case of a member or manager who mismanages or takes advantage of the LLC.[5] This type of misconduct most often involves plundering the business assets through actual theft or other instances of draining the company's financial reserves. Not giving the company the "right of first refusal" also falls under this category.

Other fraudulent acts, such as "doctoring" the business's balance sheets, may result in personal liability as well. In such situations, the individual can be sued by the LLC and will be subject to personal financial liability for losses to the company. In addition to actual damages, punitive damages may also be assessed, and the party may be subject to criminal prosecution.

Under this same heading, it is important to realize that professional service associations do not enjoy the same advantage of limited liability as other types of corporations. Michigan law does allow professional practitioners to form limited liability companies.[6] Two or more doctors or lawyers who organize their practice as an LLC, for example, will still be personally liable for any acts of professional misconduct, including malpractice, in his or her individual role as a practitioner of the profession.

Of course, everyone knows and understands this principle of personal responsibility for one's misdeeds underlying any type of professional practice. The crucial issue is whether the business form of the limited liability company will shield you from liability for misconduct on the part of *your associates, the other members of the LLC.* If you are a doctor practicing with a group of other doctors as a limited liability company and one of your associates amputates the wrong leg of a patient during surgery, are you also potentially liable for his act of misconduct? Apparently not, under the Michigan law governing LLCs. This and other important issues of professional practices organized as LLCs will be

---

5   We are not speaking here of honest errors of judgment but of gross negligence and downright intent to defraud.

6   Professions authorized by the Michigan statutes include doctors, veterinarians, dentists, public accountants, psychologists, engineers, architects, and other licensed professionals.

examined in detail in Chapter 6 ("The Michigan Professional Limited Liability Company").

Third, creditors such as banks naturally wish to limit their risks as much as possible. An owner of a small business will often be asked to pledge personal assets as security for a loan. Obviously, the shield for personal assets which the LLC form provides in other situations will not work in this case, whenever you sign a legal document agreeing to *personal* responsibility for a business loan.

In spite of these three important exceptions, the LLC does offer a limitation of liability not available to the sole proprietor or the partnership.[7] In the event of legal damages you must pay, due to injury or loss to consumers caused by goods or services you manufacture or sell, your limited liability company will serve as a reliable umbrella, in most cases protecting your personal assets from attachment and liquidation. This advantage alone may be worth the price of organizing your business as an LLC for most individuals.

The Limited liability company as a tax shelter

To answer the question of what form of business will save you the most taxes, you need to analyze your current financial situation. What individual tax bracket do you and other proposed business owners (if any) fall into? If you organize your business as a sole proprietorship, a partnership, or a limited liability company, your business income will be taxed at your personal, individual rate(s). The corporate form of business, on the other hand, has a separate rate of tax unique to that type of business organization. The federal corporate tax rate is a graduated, four-tiered rate. The first $50,000 of corporate income is taxed at 15 percent, the next $25,000 at 25 percent, the next $25,000 at 34 percent, and amounts from $100,000 to 335,000 are taxed at 39 percent. (Corporations with income of at least $335,000 pay a flat tax rate of 34 percent.)

If you form a limited liability company, the income (or loss) will flow to you directly and will be taxed at your individual rate. If you have other income, whether from a job, from certificates of deposit, and so on, all these sources of income will be lumped with the income from the LLC and taxed accordingly. You may need to sit down with a tax adviser and review your income picture reflected in your tax returns for the past several years and the projected income from the LLC, to determine whether the LLC form will save you taxes or not. Are you in a low or a high individual tax bracket at present? If, for example, you are in the highest individual federal tax bracket (39.6 percent), your LLC income will be taxed at the same rate. In such a case, the corporate form might even save you taxes if the in-

---

7   As already noted, these same limitations of personal liability would also be available to corporations. See our publication titled *How to Form Your Own Michigan Corporation Before the Inc. Dries!*

come from the business will not exceed $100,000 for the foreseeable future.

If you are in a lower individual tax bracket, on the other hand, your LLC income will be taxed at that low rate as well. For the smallest businesses with annual profits under $50,000, the tax rate of an LLC will either be the same as a corporation or somewhat higher, since the lowest personal tax rate and the lowest corporate rate are the same (15 percent) up to $23,350 in income. At that point, the personal rate goes up to 28 percent for income above $23,350 but below $56,550. The corporate rate remains at 15 percent for the first $50,000 in income. Once your business is generating annual profits above the $100,000 threshold, the LLC format should save you increasingly larger sums of taxes.

The reason for these tax savings in the case of middle-sized businesses organized as LLCs results from the unique tax requirements of regular (C) corporations. If you organize as a C corporation, you will have to pay dividends to your shareholders once your accumulated earnings in the business approach $250,000 ($150,000 for professional service corporations). Those dividends are taxed *twice,* at the corporate and the individual recipient's tax level. With an LLC, you can annually divide up the profits among the members and have them be taxed only once, at the individual members' tax rates. In a situation such as this, an LLC can save a lot of taxes for the simple reason that the C corporation is the only business form that faces a tax on accumulated earnings.

What if you and another individual are interested in setting up a business and one of you is in the highest individual tax bracket and the other is in the lowest? It may be possible to exploit this discrepancy in personal tax rates by having more of the income flow to the person with the lower tax rate, provided you organize as an LLC. This creative approach to profit allocation is not an option with an S corporation or a regular corporation. You will need to explore this possibility with a competent tax adviser.

Fringe benefits. LLCs, like S corporations, give up a number of fringe benefits available to regular corporations in exchange for pass-through tax treatment. The main fringe benefits that LLCs share with corporations is that of retirement plans. In the past, corporate retirement plans were more favorable taxwise than plans available to other types of businesses. The 1982 tax act in effect eliminated the past favoritism of corporate retirement plans over Keogh plans for the self-employed sole proprietor or the retirement plans for partners of a partnership or members of a limited liability company. The tax shelter advantages of all such plans remain immense.

In Chapter 4, we will examine in more detail the potential tax advantages of LLCs, including tax-sheltered retirement vehicles as well as medical reimbursement plans and other allowable business deductions.

Example 1 below shows how large federal income tax savings may be realized through a limited liability company, as opposed to a regular (C) corporation. Example 2 compares the same tax situation in the case of a limited liability company and an S corporation.

Example 1

The Gold family, Wanda, Junior and Giesela, run a profitable landscaping business, The Garden of Eden, in a tony suburb of Ann Arbor. The business is organized as a C corporation and earned $380,000 in profits on sales of 3 million in 1995. The corporate entity itself would pay a flat tax of 34 percent on the profits, that is, a federal tax of $129,200. Since theirs is a highly profitable company, it has to pay out a portion of its earnings each year to the 3 shareholders, Wanda, Junior, and Giesela, in the form of dividends. Because each of the members of the Gold family is in the highest personal tax bracket, each pays an additional 39.6 percent of their salary and dividend checks from the company to the federal government each year, on top of the corporate rate of 34 percent.[8]

For tax-related issues and other reasons which will be examined later, the limited liability company structure is ideal for this type of medium-sized business. Very large companies that need access to a public capital market, that is, who need to publicly sell shares of their stock, are traditionally organized as C corporations. There would be no tax advantage for a limited liability company in this big league, since the company, if it issues public shares, would automatically be taxed as though it were a C corporation even if it is organized as a limited liability company. On the other hand, the smallest companies may not enjoy any substantial tax advantages either, if organized as an LLC, as opposed to a corporate format.

See what happens to the tax picture if our hypothetical company, The Garden of Eden, were organized as a limited liability company instead of a C corporation. First and foremost, it would pay no federal entity tax, which amounted to a whopping $129,200 in our example above. The three member-owners would only pay the tax on their individual share of the profits. In other words, if the profits of $380,000 were divided up equally among the three, it would pass through the limited liability company *with no tax at the federal level.* Each of the three would receive roughly $126,667 and would show that amount on the federal 1040 tax return and be taxed at the rate of 39.6 percent of that amount.

Example 2

Your S corporation shows a profit of $49,000 for the tax year. You and your business partner are its sole shareholders. Since the S corporation is a pass-through tax entity, your portion and your partner's

---

8   The Golds' salaries are only taxed once, at their individual rate, but their dividends are taxed twice, at the corporate and the individual rate. Dividends prove much more expensive to the business operating as a corporation, since they come out of after-tax earnings.

24

portion of the profits will be taxable at your respective individual rates.

If either of you fall into the lowest tax bracket, you will pay 15 percent of your share of the $49,000 in federal taxes. Perhaps your partner files separately, and she is in the highest tax bracket. Her portion of the $49,000 would be taxed at her rate of 39.6 percent, therefore.

Say, you and your partner organize your business as a limited liability company instead of an S corporation. The profits, as in the case of the S corporation, would again flow directly to the two members, you and your partner. On the surface, there would not appear to be any tax advantage to an LLC over a S corporation.

But there is an important exception that arises if you wish to allocate the percentage of profits each of you receives in a proportion different from your relative ownership. With the S corporation you have no flexibility in this area. If you own 60 percent of the shares of the business and your partner holds 40 percent, the profits have to be divvied up in the same ratio: 6 to 4. With an LLC, you can be more creative since it is not tied to the relative proportion of ownership rights in carving up the profit pie.

An example will illustrate the significance of this advantage under certain circumstances. Rock and Gwendolyn decide to start a referral business providing part- or full-time companions for the elderly. Gwendolyn lays out almost all the cash necessary to get started: she rents an office and buys phone and fax machines and pays for advertising in local publications and the mailing of flyers.

Rock is cash-poor (he contributes only 10 percent of the startup costs) but skill-rich. He has many contacts with area organizations providing services for the elderly as well as strong interpersonal skills. His contribution to the business consists, therefore, almost exclusively of the services he can offer. He interviews prospective clients, whose names he obtains from his contacts, as well as members of a designated pool of potential companions, consisting of nursing and social services college students as well as retired but able-bodied adults.

Rock and Gwendolyn determine that the ratio of Gwendolyn's money to the value of Rock's services (plus his small cash contribution) is 1 to 1, in other words, the value of Gwendolyn's and Rock's respective contributions make them each 50 percent owners in the business.

However, because of the far greater risk that Gwendolyn assumes by making a large initial cash outlay, in light of possible failure of the enterprise, they agree that Gwendolyn should receive two ownership shares for each of Rock's shares. This kind of flexible allocation that allows for multiple types of owner contributions, different levels of risk, and rewards for unusual effort and/or creativity, is not possible with an S corporation, which would have to follow the 50/50 allocation formula based on the ratio of the assessed value of the two owner's contributions. By contrast, this arrangement is perfect with an LLC.

We have withheld several key pieces of information in this scenario in order to dramatize certain points. Rock and Gwendolyn are married but file separate tax returns. Gwendolyn does not currently work apart from her involvement in the new business. The cash that she put up came from a recent inheritance, owing to her favorite uncle who died childless and spouseless. Rock has a high-paying, high-pressure job with a major corporation. Through careful structuring of the business start-up, Gwendolyn will get a much larger share of the profits taxed at her lower (15 percent) personal rate. Rock is in the highest (39.6 percent) tax bracket. With the money they save in taxes this year, they plan to make a down payment on a country cottage, as part of their long-term plan of eventually escaping the rat race.

The above examples illustrate some of the strategies made possible by the unique structure of limited liability companies. These types of issues will be discussed further in Chapter 4, "Taxes and the Michigan Limited Liability Company."

The Basic structure of a limited liability company

The Internal Revenue Services defines corporations as business entities that possess four essential characteristics:

- continuity of life
- free transferability of interests
- centralized management
- limited liability

The IRS uses these same four characteristics as a basis for defining a limited liability company as well. However, it recognizes a limited liability company by the fact that it possesses no more than two of the above four characteristics. If the LLC has three or more of these characteristics, it will be treated as a corporation for tax purposes. Chapter 2 will look at this issue of the defining characteristics of an LLC in detail, since it is important that you organize your LLC in such a way that it will not later be called into question by the IRS and forced to be redefined as a corporation. Such a redefinition, needless to say, would involve considerable confusion and wasted effort and higher taxes in some cases. It is crucial, therefore, to determine what form of business is most advantageous for you and to be sure that you organize your business properly to obtain the results you want.

The one corporate characteristic that virtually every LLC will want to have is, of course, limitation of personal liability. So it is simply a matter of following the rules regarding the other three characteristics to be sure that your company does not possess more than one additional characteristic, which may be **either** centralized management, **or** free transferability of interests, **or** continuity of life.

Capitalizing the limited liability company

The only means that LLCs have at their disposal to raise money is through the investment of its members. In this respect, it does not differ from a small corporation whose working capital must come from its shareholder(s). Just as a closely held corporation can issue and sell additional shares of stock at any time to raise more capital, the members of the LLC can make new infusions of capital into the business, as needed.

The one avenue that an LLC does not have available to raise funds that a corporation does is the public stock markets. Most corporations never reach the size and rate of growth needed to "go public." If your dream is to have someday a company trading on a listed stock exchange, then you may very well want to organize your business as a corporation instead of an LLC. Most small companies will not achieve the magnitude of growth and be able to pay the large expenses involved of going public, however. Consequently most small companies will do fine operating as an LLC.

If you organize as an LLC and surprise yourself and everyone else by your phenomenal sales record, there is even a way of getting around the prohibition against making a public stock offering. At that point, the IRS will simply redefine your company as a corporation for tax purposes, even though you call yourself a limited liability company. This "redefinition" will involve, in most cases, paying more taxes, since corporations are subject to a double tax at both the corporate entity level and the individual shareholder level. That is the price you pay for the ability to sell shares of your company in the open market.

SUMMARY: MAJOR ADVANTAGES AND DISADVANTAGES OF LLCS

Advantages

1. There are no limitations on the number, character, and identity, of the members of a limited liability company, unlike an S corporation. Individuals, as well as other legal entities such as partnerships and corporations, can be members of an LLC. Individual members of LLCs, furthermore, do not have to be U.S. citizens. This is not the case with S corporations, whose limited liability shield and pass-through tax structure most resemble LLCs.

2.. The tax and ownership limitations of corporations are especially visible in the case of medium-sized businesses, giving LLCs a decided edge. LLCs prove more attractive tax-wise than C corporations, because they pay no federal corporate level tax and more attractive structurally than S corporations, because they have no limitation on the number of owners, often a crucial point in medium-sized businesses.

3. The tax treatment of a buyout of an owner's interests in the business impacts the remaining owners in a much more favorable way in the case of LLCs than corporations. The LLC may deduct that portion of the redemption price assignable to good will and accounts receivable. With corporations, no such tax advantage accrues to the remaining shareholders.

4. LLCs can flexibly allocate profits in a way not tied to the owners' respective investments in the business and past allocation percentages. This flexibility promotes good business practice, allowing the company to reward highly motivated and

productive individuals. In a corporation, whether a regular (C) corporation or an S corporation, profit payouts are mechanically linked to each individual owners's percentage of capital outlays.

5. Owners of LLCs may also agree to allocate losses among themselves in a way not tied to their pro rata share of investment in the company and departing from the agreed-upon rules for allocating profits. This flexibility in allocating losses can produce considerable tax benefits. This flexible method of loss allocation is not available to corporations.

6. With regard to the tax effects of distributions, owners of S corporations and LLCs alike enjoy advantages over owners of C corporations, who pay a double tax. LLC owners realize a particular tax advantage in the case of distributions of property that appreciate in value, since the corporate shareholders as well as the corporate entity must generally pay a tax on the distribution. The members of an LLC escape this double tax when distributing appreciated property.

7. When an individual receives an ownership interest in a business through the contribution of property, he often realizes a taxable gain on his individual tax return in the case of a corporation. There is never an immediate taxable gain in the case of an LLC, however.

8. Unlike a corporation, the limited liability company is not liable for unemployment tax, Social Security tax, or Medicare tax, or for any withholding from the owners. This important difference results in both tax savings as well as time savings, with less tax forms to file.

9. An LLC never pays federal income tax, whereas a C corporation does. Ordinarily, an S corporation parallels the LLC in this respect and pays no federal corporate-level tax. However, there are important exceptions in the case of S corporations that started their existence as C corporations and later switched that may trigger a federal corporate tax.

10. If the members of an LLC decide later that they want to convert the business to a corporation, they generally may do so tax-free.

11. In order for an LLC to be taxed as a partnership entity, no special elections or formal agreements are needed. Simply organizing the limited liability company in the proper way suffices. The corporation seeking tax treatment as a partnership (an S corporation election), on the other hand, requires unanimous shareholder approval and a timely filing of Form 2553 with the IRS during the first 2 and one-half months of the current tax year. Once an LLC qualifies for partnership tax status, it will automatically continue to qualify until the entity is dissolved. An S corporation poses considerably more risk in this area because it may lose its partnership tax status, advertently or inadvertently, in a host of complex ways.

12. The capital structure of an LLC is flexible. It shares this attribute with C corporations, in opposition to S corporations, which have much less flexibility in their limitation to a single class of stock.

13. The transfer of part of an ownership interest in the business to a trust for estate planning purposes is permitted in the case of an LLC; not so for S corporations.

14. In Michigan, an LLC is easily formed by filing articles of organization with the Secretary of State and paying a $50 fee.

15. In the case of bankruptcy or a lawsuit, LLCs enjoy the same limitation of personal liability as corporations.

Disadvantages

1. LLCs are more "fragile" than corporations and automatically dissolve upon significant ownership changes. If 50 percent or more of the total interests in capital and profits of an LLC are sold or exchanged within a 12-month period, regardless of whether the sale or exchange is made to an outsider or to another member, the LLC entity terminates. Steps can be taken to see that this dissolution is avoided or, if it does occur, to restore the business operations.

2. Under the Michigan statutes, an LLC requires a minimum of two persons to form, although a way around this requirement will be explained in Chapter 3. Pending final approval, the IRS plans to let one-person LLCs choose whether to be taxed as a sole proprietor or as a corporation, simply by checking a box. This ability of the one-member LLC to choose the tax status of the business proves, in fact, to be a decided advantage.

3. An LLC does not qualify for ordinary loss treatment under Section 1244, like a corporation. This provision of the tax code allows the small business corporation shareholder, if he realizes a loss upon selling or exchanging his stock, to deduct up to $50,000 ($100,000 for a husband and wife filing jointly) annually. Although this deduction is not available to LLC members, in reality this limitation is offset by the greater ability of LLC members, as opposed to corporate owners, to deduct their share of the entity's losses in the year the losses occur on their personal tax returns.

4. In medium-sized C corporation businesses that are not throwing off enough profits to have to pay dividends subject to the double tax, there is often a tax advantage for the shareholder-owners that stems from the way regular corporations are taxed. It is frequently possible to split income between the corporation and the individual owners in a way that saves taxes. This strategy is not available to an LLC. With the LLC, all the profits will be divided up annually among the members, which may very well push their income into the highest tax bracket. With a C corporation, some of the income can be paid to the shareholder-owners as salaries, while some may be kept in the business as retained earnings subject to lower corporate rates.

5. Because of the newness of the state and federal laws governing LLCs, some serious issues surrounding this business entity have not been fully spelled out. For the most part, the ambiguous issues are highly technical ones that will not affect the smaller business. Medium-sized and larger businesses adopting LLC status will want to work closely with a legal practitioner skilled in this area.

6. Corporations continue to enjoy certain fringe benefits not available to other types of businesses, including the limited liability company. This disadvantage will have to be weighed against the tax and other advantages, particularly in the case of medium-sized companies that may realize substantial tax savings from doing business as an LLC.

7. Corporate retirement plans are now more on a par with those of other business entities, but some inequalities still remain. For example, retirement plan contributions for a corporate owner may create a net operating loss for the business; this is not permissible for an LLC member. Today, there is little difference between corporate and noncorporate pension and profit-sharing plans.[9] But corporate defined benefit plans often offer better retirement benefits than those available under a noncorporate (Keogh) plan.[10]

8. Unlike the corporate owner, LLC members may not borrow from their retirement plans.

---

9   <u>Book Resource </u>The P. Gaines Co. publishes a book on setting up a corporate or noncorporate pension plan, entitled *Five Easy Steps to Setting Up an IRS-Approved Retirement Plan for Your Small Business (Incorporated or Unincorporated), With Forms.* See the order form in the back of this book.

10   See Chapter 4 for a discussion of the different types of retirement plans available.

9. The corporate owner more easily qualifies for lump-sum treatment of retirement plan funds than the LLC member.

10. Unlike a corporate owner, an LLC member may not receive a tax-free employee death benefit up to $5,000.

11. Unlike a corporate owner, an LLC member may not have premiums for group term life insurance under $50,000 paid for by the business as a tax-free fringe benefit.

12. The transfer of the rights of an LLC membership interest has certain limitations, unlike corporate shares, which are freely transferable (except in the case of closely held corporations). Whereas financial rights of LLC membership interests are generally freely transferable, governance rights are transferable only upon approval of a defined percentage of the other members (usually a majority or an unanimity).

TO FORM AN LLC OR NOT . . .

We have given an overview of the LLC as a form of business ownership, in contrast to the sole proprietorship, the partnership, and the corporation. We have also discussed many of the key advantages and disadvantages of the limited liability company. Subsequent chapters will deal in greater detail with the various topics introduced here. Before reaching a decision in your individual case on whether or not to organize an LLC, be sure to consider all the pros and cons. Plan to consult a tax adviser and/or an attorney for guidance in your particular circumstances.

Chapter 2. THE MICHIGAN LIMITED LIABILITY COMPANY

In Chapter 1, we compared and contrasted the limited liability company with the other forms of doing business, namely, the sole proprietorship, the partnership, and the corporation. Advantages and disadvantages were spelled out. In this chapter, we will take a closer look at how a limited liability company actually works.

As previously noted, the limited liability company is a business form that combines elements of a corporation and a partnership. It is as if someone sat down one day and said, "Let's make an animal that has the appearance of a dog but the stamina of a camel—let's create a dogamel." In the case of the LLC, someone might have muttered to themselves, "Wouldn't it be nice to have a business that provides liability protection for its owner(s) like a corporation but is taxed at more favorable partnership rates?" Perhaps an attorney overheard them and got to work on this problem right away, and voila!—the first limited liability company was born.

Regardless of how the first LLC began, what is clear is that this new hybrid business entity, like a corporation and a sole proprietorship, defines itself in terms of four essential characteristics: continuity of life, free transferability of interests, centralized management, and limited liability. A corporation possesses all four of these characteristics, whereas a sole proprietorship generally possesses none. The LLC falls in the middle and must possess two or fewer characteristics to be defined as a limited liability company.

The corporation, for instance, ordinarily has a perpetual existence not tied to the life of the owner(s). If the owner(s) die(s), the business can still continue uninterrupted. The corporation also has free transferability of interest, since its stock can be sold to anyone else, without restriction, except in the case of certain closely held corporations. It ordinarily has centralized management whereby corporate officers conduct its business. Finally, and most importantly, it provides its shareholder-owners an umbrella of protection from personal liability claims.

By contrast, the sole proprietorship generally has none of these four attributes. The business automatically stops with the death of the owner. Although the business may be sold, it does not have free transferability of interest in the way a corporation does, allowing for different individuals to buy into the company through stock purchases. Furthermore, it does not ordinarily possess centralized management, since the proprietor will typically do the lion's share of the work, sometimes with the help of assistants. Finally, it never enjoys the personal liability protections of a corporation: the sole proprietor is legally responsible for all the debts of the business.

The persons who organize a limited liability company will want to be sure that the business possesses limited liability, of course. That is ordinarily the main reason for choosing an LLC over a sole proprietorship or a partnership. The LLC can have no more than one of the other three corporate attributes of continuity of life, free transferability of interests, or centralized management (otherwise, it cannot be classified as an LLC). In fact, an LLC does not need to have any of these other three characteristics unless it proves advantageous to do so. We will look at each of these elements in the course of the following discussion.

Key Definitions

On any given topic, certain key terms establish a reference point, enabling us to define the nature of the activity in question. In the case of Michigan LLCs, the following definitions prove basic:

- **Articles of Organization**
- **Limited Liability Company**
- **Foreign Limited Liability Company**
- **Member**
- **Manager**
- **Member-managed Company**
- **Manager-managed Company**
- **Membership Interest**
- **Contribution**
- **Distribution**
- **Operating Agreement**
- **Principal Office**
- **Term Company**

In legal matters, even commonly used and understood terms such as "Person" may be defined in a legal context. In this case, we will not follow that practice, defining instead only those essential terms that do not appear in common usage.

Articles of Organization. A form or document (Form 700) required to be filed with the Michigan Secretary of State or other official having custody of company records in order to organize a limited liability company in this state.

Limited Liability Company. A business entity organized under the Michigan Limited Liability Company Act [MCLA §§450.4101 et seq; MSA §§21.198(4101) et seq.] by filing Form 700 with the Michigan Secretary of State.

Foreign Limited Liability Company. An unincorporated entity organized as a limited liability company under laws other than the laws of Michigan.

Member. A person with an ownership interest in a limited liability company with the rights and obligations specified under the Michigan Limited Liability Company Act. A member ordinarily has legal authority to bind the company in the course of business.

Manager. In the case of a limited liability company with centralized management, a manager or managers may be named by the members as agents of the company, in which case a member would not be an agent of the company solely by reason of being a member. The Articles of Organization or an operating agreement would spell out the rights and obligations of the managers.

Member-managed Company. In limited liability companies without centralized management, the company is run by its members, who have the authority to bind the company. The Articles of Organization will so specify.

Manager-managed Company. In limited liability companies with centralized management, the company is run by a manager or managers and the members do not have the authority to bind the company. The Articles of Organization will so specify.

Membership interest. A member's rights in the limited liability company, including the right to receive distributions of the limited liability company's assets and any right to vote or participate in management.

Contribution. Anything of value that a person contributes to the limited liability company as a prerequisite for or in connection with membership, including cash, property, services performed, or a promissory note or other binding obligation promising to contribute cash or property, or perform current or future services.

Distribution. A transfer of money, property, or other benefit from a limited liability company to a member in the member's capacity as a member.

Operating Agreement. The agreement, which must be in writing, according to Michigan law, concerning the affairs of a limited liability company and the conduct of its business; it will define the relations among the members, managers (if any), and the limited liability company.

Principal Office. The office, whether or not in this state, where the principal executive office of a domestic or foreign limited liability company is located.

Term Company. A limited liability company in which the members have agreed to remain members until the expiration of a term specified in the Articles of Organization.

Purposes of a Limited Liability Company

The Michigan Limited Liability Company Act, effective June 1, 1993, defines the types of limited liability companies that may be set up in the state and the laws governing their conduct. It is this Act that the following discussion will highlight.

Section 450.4201 gives some sense of the broad range of purposes for which Michigan limited liability companies may be organized:

A limited liability company may be formed under this act for any lawful purpose for which a domestic corporation or a domestic partnership could be formed, except as otherwise provided in article 9 or other law.[1]

In short, any "lawful" activity may be organized in Michigan as a limited liability company, including those providing professional services.

Powers of a Limited Liability Company

The Michigan Limited Liability Company Act grants to LLCs all powers necessary and convenient, including all powers granted to general business corporations, subject to any limitations stated in its Articles of Organization, the Michigan Limited Liability Company Act, or other statutes of the state of Michigan. In essence, then, the Michigan limited liability company enjoys the same powers as Michigan corporations, except in cases where those powers are specifically limited by statute. We will review below the powers of Michigan corporations, as defined by §450.1261 of the Michigan Business Corporation Act, which spells out the particular activities Michigan corporations are authorized to engage in, noting in italics those cases in which the powers are limited by statute.

1. To have perpetual duration, unless a limited period of duration is stated in the corporation's Articles. *In this case, the Michigan Limited Liability Company Act specifically states that a limited liability company in this state cannot have perpetual existence (MCLA §450.4203). We will look at the rationale for this requirement in Chapter 5 and the best way to handle it; a 30-year duration in the case of a limited liability company is standard. This does not mean that the company will have to shut its doors after 30 years, however, as we shall see.*

2. To sue and be sued in all courts and participate in actions and proceedings, judicial, administrative, arbitrative or otherwise, in the same manner as natural persons.

3. To have and alter at pleasure a seal and use it by causing it or a facsimile to be affixed, impressed, or reproduced in any other manner. The Limited Liability Company Outfit supplied by The P. Gaines Co. (see order form in back of book) provides an official seal as part of its contents.

4. To purchase, receive, take by grant, gift, devise, bequest, or otherwise, lease as leasee, invest in, encumber, sell, exchange, transfer, or otherwise acquire, own, hold, improve, employ, use, and otherwise deal in and with, any real or personal property, or an interest therein, situated in or out of the state.

5. To sell, convey, exchange, mortgage, pledge, lease as leasor, transfer, create a security interest in, or otherwise dispose of all or any part of its property, or an interest therein, wherever situated.

6. To participate with others in any corporation, partnership, limited partnership, joint venture, or other association of any kind, or in any transaction, undertaking, or agreement.

---

1   Article 9 (§450.4901) authorizes businesses rendering professional services to form limited liability companies as well. A separate chapter is devoted to the Michigan Professional Limited Liability Company (Chapter 6).

7. To purchase, take, receive, subscribe for, or otherwise acquire, own, hold, vote, employ, sell, lend, lease, exchange, transfer, or otherwise dispose of, mortgage, pledge, use, and otherwise deal in and with, bonds and other obligations, shares, or other securities or interests issued by others, whether engaged in similar or different business, governmental, or other activities, including banking corporations or trust companies.

8. To make contracts, give guarantees, and incur liabilities; to borrow money for its purposes at such rates of interest as the corporation may determine, issue its notes, bonds, and other obligations, and secure any of its obligations by mortgage or pledge of any of its property or an interest therein, wherever situated.

9. To make donations for public welfare or for community fund, hospital, charitable, educational, scientific, civic, or similar purposes, and in time of war or other national emergency in aid thereof, without regard to specific corporate benefit.

10. To invest and reinvest its funds from time to time, to lend money, and to take and hold real and personal property as security for the payment of funds so invested or loaned.

11. To conduct business, carry on its operations, and have offices and exercise the powers granted by this act in any jurisdiction within or without the United States.

12. To elect or appoint officers, employees, and other agents of the corporation, define their duties, fix their compensation and the compensation of directors, and indemnify corporate directors, officers, employees, and agents. *In the case of Michigan limited liability companies, those authorized to conduct the business of the company are defined differently than a corporation. There is no board of directors, for instance, and the actual business of the company may either be conducted by the members of the limited liability company themselves or there may be a system of centralized management like the corporate model in which a manager or managers operate the company. In the*

next section of this chapter, we will look at this issue of management in more detail.

There exist similar provisions as corporations for indemnification in the case of limited liability companies. The limited liability company's operating agreement may limit aspects of a manager's liability and provide for indemnification of managers for judgments, settlements, penalties, fines, or expenses for acts or omissions as manager. There are three cases in which the personal liability of managers cannot be limited, which will be spelled out below.

13. To adopt, alter, or repeal corporate bylaws, including emergency bylaws, relating to the business of the corporation, the conduct of its affairs, its rights and powers and the rights and powers of its shareholders, directors, or officers. *The comparable document to bylaws in the case of limited liability companies is called the operating agreement, and its provisions may be adopted, changed, or repealed in a similar manner as corporate bylaws.*

14. To cease its corporate activities and dissolve. *Limited liability companies have similar provisions for dissolution.*

15. To pay pensions, establish and carry out pension, profit sharing, share bonus, share purchase, share option, savings, thrift, and other retirement, incentive, and benefit plans, trusts, and provisions for any of its directors, officers, and employees. *Limited liability companies may provide for the retirement of its members, managers, and employees in the same manner.*

16. To purchase, receive, take, otherwise acquire, own, hold, sell, lend, exchange, transfer, otherwise dispose of, pledge, use, and otherwise deal in and with its own shares, bonds, and other securities. *As already pointed out, limited liability companies cannot issue publicly traded shares of stock without being reclassified by the IRS as a corporation for tax purposes.*

17. To have and exercise all powers necessary or convenient to effect any purpose for which the corporation is formed. *Limited liability companies pos-*

sess the same powers that are necessary or convenient to realize their business purposes, provided that they are lawful.

THE EYES AND EARS OF THE LIMITED LIABILITY COMPANY

Since the limited liability company is a fictitious person, the actual work of the LLC must be carried on by real people. Unlike a corporation which has a complex 4-tiered structure of personnel involved at various levels in its operation, the LLC may have a very simple organization consisting of:

members

That's it! The members can play all the roles of the business from setting it up — providing financing, renting office space, and selecting the official company mascot—to running its day-to-day operations.

Some larger LLCs, on the other hand, may opt for an organizational structure that more closely parallels that of corporations. The key players of these LLCs will normally consist of:

members
managers
employees

In this case, the members' roles will closely parallel that of shareholders in a corporation since they will be providing the financing for the business and are entitled to distributions. The actual management of the corporation will be centralized, however, and conducted by professional managers instead of the members themselves. Furthermore, the day-to-day work of the LLC will probably be carried out by employees hired by the business.

Thus, the size of the LLC will, in large part, determine the level of hierarchy and the degree of division of labor required to operate it successfully. The smallest businesses organized as LLCs will simply have members who will perform all the roles, from that of manager to chief bottle washer. In contrast to a corporation, with its more rigidly defined roles, an LLC of this sort provides a looser structure whose characteristics can be defined and individually tailored to the business's needs in the Articles of Organization or the operating agreement. Businesses needing more structural organization owing to their size or the personalities of their owners can opt for a more defined form of operation with the LLC format as well.

Since you have a choice as to whether to operate your Michigan LLC as a member-based company or a manager-based company, we will look in depth at these two options now.

Management by Members

Specific laws detail the way in which Michigan LLCs managed by members shall be run. First, a Michigan LLC is automatically managed by its members, who are imbued with all the rights and responsibilities of managers, unless the Articles of Organization explicitly state that the business is to be managed by managers (MCLA §450.4401).

The business's operating agreement may restrict or enlarge the management rights and duties of any member or group of members. The operating agreement may assign particular management duties to particular members. For example, it may specify that Fred Junes will be in charge of the mail order activities of Wonder Products, L.L.C., a Michigan company, whereas John Smoth will take charge of its telemarketing duties.

Member qualifications

A person may become a member of a Michigan limited liability company by making a contribution accepted by the company. Additional qualifications or procedures for membership may be prescribed in an operating agreement.

Members—minimum number

A Michigan limited liability company shall have at least two members. A procedure for getting around this requirement and setting up a Michigan LLC with one member is explained in Chapter 3.

Liability of members

Unless otherwise provided by law or in an operating agreement, a person who is a member of a Michigan LLC is not liable for the acts, debts, or obligations of the company. Members in their roles as managers may be indemnified by the company, which will be explained later in this chapter.

Contributions of members

A promise of a member to contribute to the limited liability company must be in writing and signed by the member to be legally enforceable. Unless otherwise provided in an operating agreement, a member is obligated to the LLC to perform any enforceable promise to contribute cash or property, or to perform services, even if he or she is unable to perform because of death, disability, or other reason.

If a member does not make the required contribution of property or services, he or she is obligated, at the option of the limited liability company, to contribute cash equal to that portion of the value of the stated contribution that has not been made.

Member distributions

Distributions of cash or other assets of a limited liability company shall be allocated among the members and among classes of members in the manner provided in an operating agreement. If an operating agreement does not provide for an allocation, distributions shall be allocated on the value, as stated in the limited liability company records required to be kept, of the contributions made by each member to the extent that they have been received by the limited liability company. In the case of a corporation, distributions would always be made in proportion to the investments of the individual shareholders. In the instance of LLCs, the distributions do not have to be strictly tied to the investment percentages of the owners. They may be, and if the LLC does not spell out a distribution formula in its operating agreement, they automatically will be paid out according to the pro rata share of contributions of each member.

LLCs can award highly motivated members in a way that corporations cannot, by making distributions on the basis of merit or the achievement of specific goals, for instance. You may want to consult a legal adviser if you wish to draw up an operating agreement that awards highly motivated members, for help with the proper wording of such an agreement.

Voting rights of members

Unless otherwise provided in an operating agreement, the members of a limited liability company shall vote in proportion to their shares of distributions of the company. The members have the right to vote on all the following:

- dissolution of the LLC
- merger of the LLC
- transactions involving an actual or potential conflict of interest between a manager and the LLC
- amendment to the Articles of Organization
- election or removal of manager(s) in the case of manager-based LLCs

The Articles of Organization or the operating agreement may provide for any other voting rights of members. Unless a greater vote is required by the Michigan Limited Liability Company Act, by the Articles of Organization, or by the operating agreement, a majority vote is required to approve any matter other than the selection of managers submitted for a vote by the members.

Members' rights to obtain records

Upon written request of a member, a limited liability company must mail or make available for inspection to the member or his representative copies of the most recent annual financial statement, federal, state, and local income tax returns, and other such books and records of the company as are just and reasonable.

Assignment of membership interest

A member may assign his financial interests in a Michigan limited liability company to another individual or individuals in whole or in part. An assignment of a membership interest does not entitle the assignee to participate in the management and affairs of the company. An assignee of a membership interest in a limited liability company may become a member only if the other members unanimously consent, unless the operating agreement provides otherwise.

Member withdrawal

A member may withdraw from a limited liability company as provided in the operat-

38

ing agreement or by giving written notice to the company and to the other members at least 90 days in advance of the date of withdrawal. A withdrawing member is entitled to receive any distribution to which the member is entitled under the operating agreement. The withdrawing member is also entitled to receive as a distribution, within a reasonable time after withdrawal, the fair market value of the member's interest in the limited liability company as of the date of withdrawal, based upon the member's right to share in distributions from the limited liability company.

If the member's withdrawal violates the operating agreement, however, the withdrawing member is not entitled to the distributions that would be provided otherwise. In addition, the company may recover from the withdrawing member damages for breach of the agreement in excess of the amount that would otherwise be distributable to the withdrawing member.

Management by Managers

Larger businesses may choose to have centralized management instead of member management. In such case, the Articles of Organization must provide for management of the company by one or more managers, who may—but do not have to be—members (MCLA §450.4402). The following sections will present the rules and regulations that Michigan manager-managed LLCs must follow.

Qualifications of managers

As noted, the Articles of Organization may specify that the business of the limited liability company shall be managed by or under the authority of 1 or more managers.

The managers may, but need not be, members. The operating agreement may prescribe qualifications for managers. In addition, the operating agreement shall specify the number of managers.

Election and removal of managers

Unless otherwise provided in the operating agreement, the election of managers to fill initial positions or vacancies shall be by majority vote of the members voting in proportion to their shares of distributions of the limited liability company.

The members may remove one or more managers with or without cause, unless an operating agreement provides that managers may be removed only for cause. Removal shall be by majority vote of the members, except that the operating agreement may require a higher vote for removal without cause. Removal for cause shall be at a meeting called expressly for that purpose, and the manager or managers to be removed shall have reasonable advance notice of the charges against them and an opportunity to defend themselves at the meeting.

Authority of managers

Except as otherwise provided in an operating agreement, if the limited liability company has more than one manager, all decisions of the managers shall be made by majority vote of the managers. However, every manager is an agent of the limited liability company for the purpose of its business. The act of every manager binds the limited liability company legally, unless the manager so acting does not have the authority to act for the limited liability company in the particular matter and the person with whom he or she is dealing has knowledge of the fact that he or she has no authority.

Managerial duties and liability

A manager shall perform his or her duties in good faith, with the care an ordinarily prudent person in a like position would exercise under similar circumstances and in a manner he or she reasonably believes to be in the best interests of the limited liability company. In discharging his or her duties, the manager may rely on information believed to be reliable, including: financial statements or other financial data prepared for the company; members or employees of the limited liability company; legal advisers, public accountants, engineers, or other professionals acting within their area of expertise; a committee of managers of which he or she is not a member. A manager is not entitled to rely on any of the above named sources of information if he or she has reason to believe that the information is unreliable.

A manager is not liable for any action taken as a manager or any failure to take any action if he or she performs the duties of his or her office in compliance with these criteria.

Except as otherwise provided in an operating agreement, a manager shall account to the limited liability company and hold as trustee for it any profit or benefit derived without the informed consent of the members by the manager from any transaction connected with the conduct of winding up of the limited liability company or from any personal use by him or her of its property.

An action against a manager for failure to perform his or her duties must be initiated within 3 years after the cause of action or within 2 years after the time when the cause of action is discovered or should reasonably have been discovered by the person complaining, whichever occurs first.

Managerial breach of duty; Limitation of financial liability; Purchase of insurance

The Articles of Organization or the operating agreement may eliminate or limit the monetary liability of a manager to the limited liability company for any breach of duty. This provision does not eliminate or limit the liability of a manager for any of the following:

(1) the receipt of a financial benefit to which the manager is not entitled
(2) liability for an unlawful distribution to the member(s) of the LLC
(3) a knowing violation of law

A limited liability company may indemnify and hold harmless a manager from and against any and all losses, expenses, claims, and demands sustained by reason of any acts or omissions or alleged acts or omissions as a manager, to the extent provided for in the operating agreement or in a contract with the person or to the fullest extent permitted by law, subject to any restrictions in the operating agreement or contract. The company cannot, however, indemnify any person for conduct described in the previous paragraph.

A limited liability company may purchase and maintain insurance on behalf of a manager against any liability or expense asserted against or incurred by him or her arising our of his or her status as a manager.

Chapter 3. HOW TO FORM A ONE-PERSON LLC IN MICHIGAN

As already noted, the Michigan laws currently require a minimum of two persons to form a limited liability company in this state. Form 700, Articles of Organization for Use by Domestic Limited Liability Companies, explicitly requires a minimum of two persons to sign the document. Otherwise, the Michigan Department of Commerce will not accept it for filing. Perhaps you are a single person engaged in a business for profit or one who is planning to start a business in the near future. After weighing the different available business formats—the sole proprietorship, the partnership, the corporation, and the limited liability company—you have a strong preference for the LLC because of its ease of setting up and running as well as its liability protection.

Fine. What do you do now—beat the bushes for a business associate, hang out at singles bars until you meet someone, or simply forget the whole idea of an LLC? There is a little known device for operating as an LLC in Michigan without coming up with a second person (or listing your dog as the second member). This chapter will explain the procedure for establishing a one-person LLC in Michigan.

First of all, you do not have to organize your business in the state where you reside.

This trick of forming the business in a state with more favorable laws is used frequently by larger corporations. While we don't normally recommend such an approach for a smaller company unless there is a good reason for it, in this case there is. The procedure is relatively simple and inexpensive.

States that currently authorize one-person LLCs include Texas, Arkansas, Pennsylvania, Idaho, Indiana, Montana, New Hampshire, and Delaware. In time, more states are expected to follow suit and grant individuals acting alone the right to form LLCs, since there is no tax or legal reason for not allowing it. A few years down the road, the state of Michigan will likely authorize one-person LLCs. In the meantime, here's the secret to setting up a one-person LLC in Michigan at present.

Three Steps to Forming a One-person LLC in Michigan

The three steps you will need to follow to set up a one-person LLC in Michigan are these:

Step One: File Articles of Organization for an LLC in one of the states listed above that allow one-person LLCs.

Step Two: **File as a foreign LLC in Michigan.**

Step Three: **Hire a registered agent in the state that you formed your one-person LLC in, who will give you a legal mailing address in that state.**

We will walk you through these steps.

Step One. We recommend that single Michigan residents wishing to form an LLC do so in Delaware, given the simplicity of LLC laws and low fees in that state. A sample filled-in Delaware Certificate of Formation[1] appears on the following page. A blank copy of this form is also included in Appendix E. Fill in the form following the example and submit the form with a one- time filing fee of $70 to the Delaware Division of Corporations, whose mailing address appears hereafter:

State of Delaware
Division of Corporations
PO Box 898
Dover, Delaware 19903
Telephone: (302) 739-3073

Step Two. Fill in the form registering your business as a foreign LLC in Michigan (Form 760) and submit the form, with a $50 fee to the Michigan Department of Commerce, whose address is shown on the form. A sample filled-in version of this form appears in this chapter. A blank copy of this form is included in Appendix E.

Step Three. Hire a registered agent to give you a legal mailing address in Delaware. Any business organized in a state where the owner(s) have no physical presence in the form of an office or store must have a contact person situated in the state. You can request a complete list of registered agents operating in the state by calling the Delaware Corporation Division, whose phone number appears in the previous paragraph. One company that provides this service is The Corporation Co. They can be contacted in Michigan at the following number: (810) 646-9033.

The annual fee that this particular company currently charges for this service is $155. You can call several of the companies on the list provided by the state of Delaware to see if you can find a cheaper rate. In addition to giving you a legal mailing address in the state, the registered agent will mail to you all official correspondence from the Delaware Secretary of State. These might consist of tax forms, notification of law changes, or legal papers in the case of a lawsuit that might arise against your company.

If you follow the above three-step procedure to form a one-person Michigan LLC, the state of Michigan, interestingly enough, will never know that you are a one-person LLC. It's all perfectly legal and simply allows you to bypass a troublesome regulation which may very well be overturned by

---

1   Most states refer to the document that you file in order to obtain legal recognition of your LLC as
     Articles of Organization. Delaware and a few other states such as New Jersey call it by a different
     name, a Certificate of Formation.

STATE *of* DELAWARE
LIMITED LIABILITY COMPANY
CERTIFICATE *of* FORMATION

▶ **FIRST:** The name of the limited liability company is ___**Gold Enterprises, L.L.C.**___

___

▶ **SECOND:** The address of its registered office in the State of Delaware is ___33609 Lazarus Lane___ ___ in the City of ___Dover___ , County of ___Kent___ . The name of its Registered Agent at such address is ___Angela Fritzlemon___

___

▶ **THIRD:** (Use this paragraph only if the company is to have a specific effective date of dissolution: "The latest date on which the limited liability company is to dissolve is ___December 31, 2030___ .")

▶ **FOURTH:** (Insert any other matters the members determine to include herein.)

___

___

___

___

___

___

▶ **IN WITNESS WHEREOF,** the undersigned have executed this Certificate of Formation of ___**Gold Enterprises, L.L.C.**___ this day of ___January 1___ , 19 ___97___ .

Wanda Gold
___
Authorized Person(s)

___

___

MICHIGAN DEPARTMENT OF COMMERCE - CORPORATION AND SECURITIES BUREAU	
Date Received:	(FOR BUREAU USE ONLY)

Name	
Wanda Gold	
Address	
920 Moose Road	

City	State	Zip Code
Dexter, Michigan		48130

EFFECTIVE DATE:

✌ Document will be returned to the name and address you enter above ✌

L	C		–			

APPLICATION FOR CERTIFICATE OF AUTHORITY
TO TRANSACT BUSINESS IN MICHIGAN
For use by Foreign Limited Liability Companies
(Please read information and instructions on last page)

Pursuant to the provisions of Act 23, Public Acts of 1993, the undersigned limited liability company executes the following Application:

1. The name of the limited liability company is:

   Gold Enterprises, L.L.C.

2. (Complete this item only if the limited liability company name in item 1 is not available for use in Michigan.) The assumed name of the limited liability company to be used in all its dealings with the Bureau and in the transaction of its business in Michigan is:

3. It is organized under the laws of _____Delaware_____.

   The date of its organization is _____January 1, 1997_____.

   The duration of its existence is until _____December 31, 2030_____.

4. The address of the office required to be maintained in the state of organization or, if not so required, the principal office of the limited liability company is:

33609 Lazarus Lane	Dover, Delaware		19902
(Street Address)	(City)	(State)	(ZIP Code)

45

5. a. The address of its registered office in Michigan is:

<u>920 Moose Road,</u>   <u>Dexter</u> , Michigan <u>48130</u>
(Street Address)   (City)   (ZIP Code)

  b. The mailing address of the registered office if different than above:

<u>same</u> , Michigan <u>   </u>
(P.O. Box)   (City)   (ZIP Code)

  c. The name of the resident agent at the registered office is:

<u>Wanda Gold</u>

---

6. The Department is appointed the agent of the foreign limited liability company for service of process if no agent has been appointed, or if appointed, the agent's authority has been revoked, the agent has resigned, or the agent cannot be found or served through the exercise of reasonable diligence.

The name and address of a member or manager or other person to whom the administrator is to send copies of any process served on the administrator is:

<u>Wanda Gold</u>
(Name)

<u>920 Moose Road,</u>   <u>Dexter, Michigan</u>   <u>48130</u>
(Street Address)   (City)   (State)   (ZIP Code)

---

7. The specific business which the limited liability company is to transact in Michigan is as follows:

The business will conduct public seminars on financial planning.

The limited liability company is authorized to transact such business in the jurisdiction of its organization.

Signed this <u>20</u> day of <u>January</u> , 19 <u>97</u>

By <u>Wanda Gold</u>
(Signature)

<u>Wanda Gold</u>   <u>Member/Chief Executive Officer</u>
(Type or Print Name)   (Type or Print Title)

the Michigan state legislature at some point in the future. It will cost you a one-time fee of $70 to set up the out-of-state LLC, the annual fee of $155 to have a Delaware registered agent on an ongoing basis, and a $100 annual registration fee to the state of Delaware But that may be a small price to pay to have the type of business entity ideally suited to your needs.

Tax Angle of One-person LLCs

One problem with the one-person LLC has been the uncertainty regarding its tax status. The IRS has now clarified how it will classify one-person LLCs for tax purposes, pending final approval. You have a choice which you can make by simply checking a box: the one-person LLC will be taxed as either a federal corporation or a sole proprietor.

Since a sole proprietor pays taxes according to his or her individual rate, a one-person LLC would pay taxes in the same way. The income and deductions of a single-member LLC whose owner is an individual person will be reported on a Schedule C of the individual's Form 1040.

You may also choose the option of having your single-member LLC taxed as a corporation. For businesses with annual profits under $100,000, it may not make a whole lot of difference how the entity is taxed. The corporate rate will, in some instances, actually be lower than the individual rate. You should review your individual case with a tax adviser to determine how best to handle the option of which road to take, whether to be taxed on the federal level as a corporation or as a sole proprietor. Presumably, your state taxing authority will follow the same path and tax the single-member LLC in the same manner as the federal government. Michigan is unique in that it charges every business of a certain size, regardless of its form, the same tax rate (the Single Business Tax). See Chapter 4, pages 48-49, for details.

Chapter 4. TAXES AND THE MICHIGAN LIMITED LIABILITY COMPANY

One of the biggest issues that molds any business decision is the tax angle. The limited liability company is no exception. Because of the importance of this subject, we have suggested that you meet with a tax adviser to review your business plans. This will help you to determine if the limited liability company or some other business structure will prove most favorable taxwise in your particular situation.

In this chapter we will look at the broad tax picture of a Michigan limited liability company. There are, for instance, certain Michigan taxes that affect all businesses in this state, regardless of their formal structure, such as the Michigan Single Business Tax, sales taxes, and unemployment and workers' compensation taxes. We will consider these taxes under the rubric of the limited liability company, as well as other tax-related and tax-savings matters, such as retirement plans.

We have seen how the limited liability company, in a nutshell, is a pass through tax entity. That is, its profits and losses accede to the individual member-owners and appear on their personal income tax returns (state and federal). This basic characteristic of LLCs is fairly straightforward and easy

to understand. Certain less obvious attributes of LLCs with important tax ramifications, such as the special tax considerations of buying into an LLC with either the offer of property or services to be performed in the future, will be looked at as well.

Michigan State Taxes

Michigan Single Business Tax

In 1975, the state of Michigan adopted an innovative type of tax structure termed the "Single Business Tax." This tax was intended to provide an incentive for new investment as well as create a more stable source of revenue and distribute the business tax over a broader base of businesses than previously. Seven taxes were repealed with the enactment of the Single Business Tax: Michigan corporation income tax, corporation franchise privilege fee, financial institutions income tax, savings and loan association privilege fee, domestic insurance companies privilege fee, property tax on inventories, and intangibles tax on business. The Single Business Tax is not an income tax, measured by income or profits; it is based on the economic size or "value-

48

added" of a business activity for the tax year. All individuals conducting a business activity in Michigan whose gross receipts for tax year 1996 exceed $250 thousand must file an annual return.

The Single Business Tax is a modified value added tax on the use of labor and capital in the business activity. The tax is calculated according to three major components: the amount of profits, compensation, and interest paid. This tax base is then reduced by the purchase of depreciable property during the tax year, as well as by various other deductions and credits. The tax rate is currently 2.3 percent of the adjusted tax base. The tax rate is computed the same way for all types of businesses, whether sole proprietors, partnerships, corporations, or limited liability companies. Of the approximately 400,000 businesses in Michigan, about 200,000 are required to file Single Business Tax returns each year.

State sales tax

Both incorporated and unincorporated Michigan businesses are required to pay sales taxes to the state, collected on retail sales. It is actually the consumer, not the business, who pays these taxes, but you as a business owner-operator are responsible for collecting the taxes in an orderly fashion and remitting them to the state at regular intervals. The Michigan sales tax rate is currently 6 percent of the amount of the retail sale. You will need to file for a Michigan sales tax permit prior to starting business as an LLC. This permit will assign your business its own individual sales tax I.D.

Individual state income tax

Any profits distributed to the individual members of the limited liability company during the year must be reported on the state personal income tax returns of the recipients. These profits are taxed at the rate of all personal income in Michigan, presently a rate of 4.4 percent (down from 5.1 percent previously). This tax rate is subject to certain tax credits, including a property tax credit, which gives the most tax relief to senior citizens, the disabled, blind persons, and disabled veterans or the surviving spouse of a veteran; a home heating credit; a farmland preservation credit; and a solar energy credit.

Michigan unemployment compensation tax

One important tax question that arises is, Are LLC members in Michigan subject to state unemployment tax on distributions? General partners in a partnership generally do not fit under the IRS' definition of an employee. LLC members who have a say in the management of the limited liability company do not fit either, according to Michigan law. Therefore, distributions to them would not be subject to Michigan unemployment tax.

An important exception: if the LLC employs non-member managers, however, they would be considered employees of the business and would be subject to state unemployment tax on any remunerations received by them from the business.

State workers' compensation tax

Workers' compensation is a form of insurance. Workers' compensation insurance set by state law covers any claims for bodily injuries or job-related diseases suffered by employees in your business, regardless of fault.

Logically, you might expect that the policy regarding state unemployment compensation would apply to workers' compensation payments as well. It turns out that such is not the case. If a Michigan limited liability company has at least one full-time or three part-time employees, all member-managers are considered employees of the LLC, and the business must pay the state workers' compensation tax.

Federal Taxes

Federal filing requirement for LLCs

You will need to file annually an informational tax return with the IRS for your LLC, but no tax will be due. At present, no form is custom designed for the LLC filing. You must use IRS Form 1065, the partnership return, and include with it a completed Form 1065 Schedule K-1 for each member. On this form, you will list each member's share of LLC income, as well as credits and deductions.

Federal individual income tax

Like the State of Michigan, the federal government also taxes profits which are paid out to individual members of a limited liability company. Each member's share of profits (or losses) will be shown on Form 1040 as income and will be taxed at the individual's personal income tax rate.

At present, there are five different federal tax brackets: 15 percent, 28 percent, 31 percent, 36 percent, and 39.6 percent. Your tax bracket depends on (1) the amount of income you show for the year and (2) your filing status. There are five filing statuses: single, married filing jointly, married filing separately, head of household, and qualifying widow(er).

As previously pointed out, the limited liability company is the most flexible business entity when it comes to allocating income among its owners. The next section will consider how you can actually divide income in such a way that, in the case of family members who are co-owners of the business, those in the lowest tax brackets can receive the lion's share of income taxed at their lower rates.

Federal unemployment tax

As noted previously in regard to Michigan unemployment tax, general partners in a partnership arrangement are ordinarily exempt. Therefore, limited liability company member-managers would be exempt from federal unemployment tax as well. Non-member managers would be considered employees of the LLC, however, and would be subject to the federal unemployment tax on any distributions they receive. Note: the owner of a single-member LLC which opts to be taxed as a corporation would be liable for the tax.

50

Determining Individual Members' Share of Profits or Losses for Tax Purposes

As you have no doubt become aware by now, the LLC is much more flexible than a corporation when it comes to allocating profits and losses. In many cases, there may be no need for any kind of fancy allocation formula. Say, you have a husband and wife owned and managed LLC, with each contributing 50 percent of the capital to set up the business. You may be perfectly happy splitting the profits or losses down the middle as well, 50/50. But—and this is an important but—if there are tax advantages to having a different profit or loss allocation, you basically can do whatever you please, *as long as you have a tax adviser insert the proper technical language in your operating agreement.*

That's right. The IRS has a special term for any kind of disproportionate splitting of profits and losses in the case of a partnership or limited liability company. "Special allocation" is what it is referred to by the feds. It is the intention of the IRS that special allocations not be made simply to reduce the tax burden of the owners of a business, but that they have some economic justification as well. As we saw in a previous example, one rationale for a disproportionate allocation might be that one member is assuming more risk through cash contributions, as opposed to the service contributions of another member.

In reality, there exists a major tax loophole in this area because any special allocation will be accepted by the IRS as having an economic basis, provided the proper wording is inserted in your operating agreement, taken from Section 704(b) of the Internal Revenue Code. If you adopt these so-called safe harbor provisions in your operating agreement, there are certain effects that come into play when the business is sold or liquidated. Needless to say, this is a highly technical area. You will need to work with a tax consultant versed in the finer points of partnership tax law to take advantage of this tax loophole. Someone who stands to benefit most from special allocations of profits and losses in a limited liability company is usually a family member and co-owner of the business who is in a different tax bracket from the other owner(s).

The Ins and Outs of Michigan Business Practices

The present book focuses on how to form a limited liability company in Michigan. There are a number of business practices and procedures that all businesses in Michigan must follow, such as registration of the business with the state, which are beyond the scope of this book. These regulations that govern the formation and operation of Michigan businesses are covered in an excellent publication from Oasis Press, **Starting and Operating a Business in Michigan.** *The price of this book is $24.95, and it is available from the P. Gaines Co. See the order form in the back of this book.*

Special Tax Considerations When Property Is Contributed to Buy a Membership Interest in an LLC

Potential members of an LLC will typically offer cash as a means of buying into the company. But it is not unusual to have members who want to contribute property and/or services instead of cash. In the next two sections, we will look at some of the special tax considerations that arise as a result.

The area of property buy-ins—which may consist of land, buildings, or any other types of tangible property, such as office furniture or equipment, a truck or a boat—is one in which LLCs generally receive more favorable tax treatment than corporations. Transfers of property to corporations in exchange for a capital interest in the business frequently trigger taxes under Internal Revenue Code Section 351. With LLCs, contributions of property are usually tax-free at the time of transfer.

Depending on how much the contributed property appreciates, less or more taxes will be owed to the IRS when the member sells his interest in the LLC to someone else or the LLC itself is later sold. The difference, then, between the corporate and the LLC tax treatment of contributed property is one of timing. With the corporation, you will often have to pay a tax up front, at the time of transfer. With the LLC, the tax is deferred until a second transfer of the property to another owner-member takes place or the business itself is liquidated or sold.

An example will show how the process works. Fred owns two acres of land that he bought for $10,000. Its current value is appraised at $30,000 when he transfers it to Urban Geeks, LLC. As you can see, its value has appreciated by $20,000 since he purchased it. Owing to this transfer of the parcel of land, on which the new LLC plans to build a retail store, Fred receives a $30,000 capital interest in the company.

Fred's cost, termed his "basis," is $10,000. Somewhere down the road when the LLC is liquidated or sold or Fred sells his interest in the LLC to another person (or the remaining members), Fred will have to pay tax on his gain exceeding his basis. If he receives $30,000 for his land interest at the time of sale, Fred will have a $20,000 profit which he will have to pay taxes on ($30,000 sales price - $10,000 basis = $20,000 profit).

If you have members who wish to contribute property for a membership interest in a limited liability company, you will need to consult a tax adviser about the tax consequences. If the property is not free and clear at the time of transfer (if it has a mortgage on it, for instance, or a lien), this liability must be carried on the books of the LLC. In calculating the basis of real property, furthermore, various adjustments, such as depreciation and capital improvements, can lower or raise the basis and alter the taxable profits at the time of sale.

Special Tax Considerations When Services Are Promised to Buy a Membership Interest in an LLC

You may be surprised to learn that the IRS views the offer to perform future services for an LLC in exchange for a membership interest as a taxable transaction. The IRS considers the membership interest as a form of compensation for services (to be) performed. What this boils down to is that the member who pays for his or her interest in the LLC by means of services will have to ante up income taxes on the value of the membership.

Say you are offering $20,000 in services as your contribution to Lucky Lady, LLC, and the two other members are contributing $20,000 each in cash. You alone will have to pay tax on the services contribution, *as though you received $20,000 in payments from the LLC*.

If you are in the 15 percent tax bracket, then the tax on the $20,000 services contribution will amount to $3,000. What is likely to happen, however, is that this $20,000 in imputed income that you will owe taxes on may push you into the higher 28 percent bracket, in which case you may owe close to $6,000 in taxes on your service contribution.

This hidden tax may cause you to think twice about whether you want to offer services in lieu of money to purchase an interest in an LLC. Your initial delight at discovering how flexible LLCs are, allow-

ing someone to work for the company as a form of payment for a membership interest, may quickly give way to tax-induced despondency. If you are contributing services instead of cash to a start-up LLC, it is probably because you are shy of cash to begin with, so a large tax bill is probably going to be the last thing you want. Now that we have exposed the potential problem with this type of contribution, we can look for ways around this dilemma.

• **Alternate Route #1.** One solution may be to seek a loan from the LLC itself, other members, or a conventional source such as a bank to buy an interest in the LLC in cash. You might have an arrangement with the LLC which combines the loan with your working for the LLC as an employee. You will thereby receive cash payments for your services, part of which you can use to pay back the loan.

• **Alternate Route #2.** Instead of receiving a membership interest (a percentage of ownership) in the business in exchange for your services, you can ask for a profit interest only. This reduces your level of involvement in the business, of course, but it has the advantage of eliminating your tax bill on imputed income which you are never actually paid. Under this arrangement, you will receive an agreed on portion of the profits in exchange for your services. The payouts you receive will be taxable, but in this instance you will be getting cash to pocket from the business, part of which can be used to meet your tax obligations.

Tax-Free Deductible Fringe Benefits

Corporations do enjoy certain tax-free benefits that are not available to limited liability companies. There is a trade-off: because LLCs receive pass-through tax treatment, they are not eligible for most perks available to corporations. S corporations, by the way, are subject to basically the same limitations. Individuals who own more than 2 percent of the stock of an S corporation (any substantive owner, in other ways) cannot participate in corporate fringe benefits, which include:

• medical reimbursement plans
• tax-free term life insurance policies up to $50,000 per employee
• tax-free dividends (actually, 70 percent of the dividends received by corporations escape taxes)
• educational expenses up to $5,250 per employee
• interest-free and low-interest loans

Business owners who can take full advantage of corporate perks such as these may find that the advantages offered by incorporation outweigh other considerations.

The two main fringe benefits that LLCs enjoy are the right to set up IRA or Keogh plans and the right to deduct a portion of medical insurance premiums. (You may deduct 30 percent of health insurance premiums you paid for yourself, your spouse, and your dependents for the tax year on Form 1040, Line 26.)[1]

How to Inc. Yourself in Michigan

For those who are contemplating setting up an incorporated business in Michigan or who simply need more detailed information, please consult our publication, **How to Form Your Own Michigan Corporation Before the Inc. Dries!** *This book covers the pros and cons of incorporation in Michigan, walks the reader through the step-by-step process, and provides all needed forms in a tear-out format. This guide also provides a thorough discussion of the tax-free perks available only to corporations. See the order form in the back of this book.*

---

1   This deduction increases to 40 percent of annual health insurance premium expenses in 1997, 45 percent in 1998 through 2002, 50 percent in 2003, 60 percent in 2004, 70 percent in 2005, and 80 percent in 2006 and subsequent years Both medical and dental health insurance premiums may be deducted, as well as long-term care insurance premiums after tax year 1996.

Retirement Plans

There are two basic types of pension plans available to businesses, (1) defined contribution plans and (2) defined benefit plans. The former is much simpler to administer, because it limits the amount of actual contributions to a set dollar amount or a percentage of earnings. A member-manager of a limited liability company can make tax-free payments to a defined contribution Keogh plan. There are two formats of defined contribution plan: the profit-sharing and the money-purchase plan.[2] For the first, the profit-sharing plan, you can contribute up to 15 percent of each employee's (including the member-managers) annual compensation. With a money-purchase plan, you can contribute up to 25 percent of each employee's compensation. The maximum amount of annual contribution for each employee cannot exceed $30,000, however.

The second type of pension plan, the defined benefit plan, is more complicated to administer because it pays the retiree a specified amount during retirement. The actual dollar amount of contributions permitted each year can only be determined by an actuary.

The maximum annual retirement benefit for 1995 plan year contributions may not exceed $120,000. In other words, enough money can be put into the plan to assure that you will receive up to $120,000 a year in retirement benefits. This $120,000 limit is subject to annual inflation adjustments.

Only businesses that are very profitable should consider defined benefit pension plans because contributions have to be made proportionately to all your employees' retirement accounts. These contributions must be made every year, furthermore, regardless of whether the business is showing a profit.

Both types of plan, defined contribution and defined benefit, provide tax-deferred benefits to the member-manager and other employees of the business, if any, since the funds are allowed to accumulate tax free until withdrawal. These contributions are completely tax deductible by the recipients. If the business is dissolved, the pension funds can be rolled over tax free into IRA accounts for its owners and employees.

One very important aspect of pension plan set-asides is that such plans cannot discriminate in favor of the owner-employees. If your limited liability company has no employees working for it other than the

---

2   A money-purchase plan permits larger annual contributions, but it requires an employer to make fixed contributions each year, regardless of whether the business is profitable. The profit-sharing plan, as the name implies, need only be paid in years when the business shows a profit. It is possible to have both types of plans, which proves advantageous for many businesses, but the overall limit of 25 percent of compensation still holds. The trustee who sets up your plan, often a bank, can explain the advantage of having both types of plan.

member-managers, there appears to be no question of discrimination. Your plan must, however, provide for coverage of additional employees if and when they are hired. If your company has other employees besides the member-managers from the start, it is normally required to cover them in your pension plan as well as yourselves. Generally speaking, contributions made on behalf of the manager-owners may not exceed the ratio of contributions made on behalf of other employees. Including other employees in your retirement plan will necessarily figure as part of your overall employee compensation package.

There are also certain cases in which employees can be excluded from coverage if you so wish. If your business hires "independent contractors," you will not have to cover them in your pension or profit-sharing plans (since they are not considered employees). Part-time employees who work less than 1,000 hours a year and those under the age of 21 can generally also be excluded from coverage. Your plan may not exclude employees over a certain age.

You may want to see a tax consultant prior to setting up a pension plan for your limited liability company to insure the legality of your proposed plan as well as favorable tax treatment and maximum pension benefits. In many cases, it will be advantageous to set up a trust to receive Keogh contributions. You may name yourself or an independent trustee to oversee the trust.

Unlike a corporation which permits a trustee as well as plan participants to borrow money from its pension fund under certain conditions, you will be subject to penalties if you own more than 10 percent of the business and borrow from its pension trust.

SEPs

Another pension option especially attractive for the small business owner merits a separate discussion of its own. Simplified Employee Pensions (SEPs for short) offer a relatively new, hassle-free form of retirement plan available for **all** types of businesses, whether corporations, partnerships, sole proprietors, or member-managers of an LLC. Unlike other type of pension plans, SEPs entail no administrative expense and no burdensome paperwork.

For businesses with limited resources, SEPs are ideal retirement vehicles because of the ease of setting them up and the benefits they provide, which compare favorably with other types of defined contribution plans. They have a $30,000 annual limit or 15 percent of compensation, whichever is less. They offer flexible funding, furthermore, since they can be financed solely by the employer, solely by the employee, or a combination of the two. They also offer the advantage that they can be integrated with Social Security. Most importantly, you do not have to contribute to the plan in those years you choose not to do so, whether for financial or other reasons.

SEPs for the Masses

The P. Gaines Co. publishes a book about SEPs, **Five Easy Steps to Setting Up an IRS-Approved Retirement Plan for Your Small Business.** *Its easy-to-read text, laced with humorous illustrations, explains how any business that is even modestly profitable can establish a SEP immediately. It walks the reader through the five steps for setting up a SEP and includes* all needed forms in a tear-out format. See the order form in the back of this book.

57

Chapter 5. FORMING YOUR OWN MICHIGAN LIMITED LIABILITY COMPANY

If you have carefully read the preceding chapters and have concluded that you are one of the individuals who can benefit from the LLC form of business, you are now ready to learn about the procedure for setting up your own Michigan limited liability company. [1]

We will first consider the issue of business name selection. This is an extremely important area. We suggest, therefore, that you devote considerable energy and thoughtfulness to it. Your business name has the power to draw customers to you or repel them. If not carefully chosen, your business name also has the potential to involve you in crippling legal battles. It is a two-edged sword, so choose and use it wisely.

Limited Liability Company Name

The first step in organizing your LLC is the choice of a name for your business which effectively 'sells' the idea of your business to others and which complies with state law. The Michigan statutes specify that your LLC name must contain the designation "Limited Liability Company" or the abbreviation "L.L.C." or "L.C." (The name cannot contain the word "corporation" or "incorporated" or the abbreviation "corp." or "inc.")

Also, the name you select must be *distinguishable* from the names of all other entities and trade or assumed names as filed, registered, or reserved with the Michigan Department of Commerce, including:

(1) the name of a domestic limited liability company or a foreign limited liability company authorized to transact business in Michigan

(2) the name of a corporation subject to the Michigan Business Corporation Act or a nonprofit corporation subject to the Michigan Nonprofit Corporation Act

(3) an assumed name ("doing business as")

---

1   If you are considering forming a professional service LLC as a doctor, dentist, engineer, etc., we suggest that you read this chapter first, then Chapter 6, which deals specifically with the Michigan professional service LLC.

(4) the name of a domestic or foreign limited partnership

(5) a reserved name for future use, under the provisions of Act 284 of the Public Acts of 1972 or Act 213 of the Public Acts of 1982

Furthermore, the name you choose for your limited liability company shall not contain a word or phrase, or abbreviation or derivative of a word or phrase, that indicates or implies that the company is formed for a purpose other than the purpose or purposes permitted by its Articles of Organization. In other words, the name may not imply that the LLC is organized for a purpose that directly contradicts the purpose stated in the Articles of Organization. If you follow our recommendation and use the general purpose clause preprinted on the form without additions, you still must steer clear of using words in your name that imply affiliation with banking or insurance concerns or professional services (such as law or architecture) that you are not licensed to perform.

If you are currently running a business in the state as a sole proprietor or partner, you can use the same business name for your limited liability company as you presently have by just adding "L.L.C.," provided that another business entity from the list above is not now operating in Michigan under the same name. Even if the name you choose for your own limited liability company is your own name, you still may not be able to use it if it turns out that someone is already doing business in Michigan under the name, unless you modify it in some way to clearly distinguish your business name from the other person's. (Just because your name happens to be Ford, don't imagine that this means that you can open a Ford Motor Company, L.L.C. in Detroit. But perhaps a Ford Drug Store, L.L.C. will work, provided one is not already registered with the Michigan Department of Commerce.)

One final, very important consideration: your name cannot infringe on the rights of others, wherever situated. If you are opening a corner dry cleaning shop, then all you normally have to worry about is whether the name you choose is free and clear in Michigan. This is because the scope of your business is strictly local, confined to the community in which you live. But if you will be selling goods or providing services on a statewide or an interstate basis, the wider scope and greater visibility of your business opens you to a possible trademark or service mark infringement lawsuit.

In the event of such a lawsuit, you may have to stop using your business name and even pay monetary damages to another company. If your business activity will not be confined to your immediate locale, we highly recommend a trademark and/or trade name search of your proposed name to avoid costly litigation. The P. Gaines Co. provides this type of computerized search. Please phone 1-800-578-3853 or write for details.

The Name's The Thing

The P. Gaines Co. publishes a helpful and widely reviewed book on selecting names for use in commerce: **Naming Your Business and Its Products and Services: How to Create Effective Trade Names, Trademarks, and Service Marks to Attract Customers, Protect Your Good Will and Reputation, and Stay Out of Court!** *Every business, whether a corporation, a partnership, a sole proprietor, or a limited liability company, needs to have a business name under which it conducts its affairs. Need we point out that it is important that such a name be legal, from the standpoint of trademark law, as well as catchy. This guide will show you how to have the best of both worlds. See the order form in the back of this book.*

In the event that you do organize your business as an LLC, it is important to realize that even though the business name you select for your company is approved by the Michigan Department of Commerce, this is no guarantee of the legality of the use of the name from the standpoint of trademark law. You may still be sued by an incorporated or unincorporated company in Michigan or in another state if the name chosen is the same as, or deceptively similar to, that of the other company's.

The use of your family surname (your last name) as your business name, furthermore, is often the worst possible choice, for

several reasons. The guide book to business names referred to in the adjacent column fully explains these and other significant issues in the business name selection process, whether that of a trade name, trademark, or service mark.

You have to include the name of your limited liability company in the Articles of Organization which you file with the Department of Commerce. You may want to reserve the name you have decided on in advance, particularly if you have made your name selection but won't be filing the Articles of Organization right away. You can submit to the Department of Commerce a written application requesting the use of a specified name as the name of your LLC, along with a ten-dollar filing fee. A copy of the form which you may use to reserve your name is included in the back of this book in Appendix E. If the name specified in your application is available, you will be given the exclusive right to its use as the name of your LLC for 60 days (the reservation is also renewable).

If you are in a hurry to organize your business, the quickest procedure is to ask for a telephone confirmation of a particular name by calling 1-900-555-0031. The cost of this procedure is $1.50 per minute, but the persons working this line are very fast and usually take only a few minutes to check your name availability.

Although a telephone check is a reliable indication in most cases, it does not absolutely guarantee the availability of a particular name which is cleared in this fashion. The Department of Commerce reserves the right to make the final decision on the matter when a name reservation request has been approved or Articles of Organization have been filed.

As a necessary precaution, do not have business stationery or customized member certificates printed or make other commitments to a name until the Articles of Organization have been filed and approved.

To save time, it may be a good idea to either reserve your name in advance or at least have a preliminary name check via phone. Otherwise, your Articles will be returned to you unfiled if the name you have chosen has already been taken, and you will have to refile again under another name. . . and again . . . and again, until you hit on a name that isn't currently being used. A little foresight and advance planning will eliminate these potential delays.

The Articles of Organization

In order to obtain LLC status, you will now need to fill out and mail to the Department of Commerce one original copy (photocopied signatures not acceptable) of your Articles of Organization. This form is simple to complete in most cases. A copy of the form is found in Appendix A in the back of this book. If the form has already been removed or you have a library edition of this book whose forms are not of the tear-out variety, additional copies can be obtained from the Michigan Department of Commerce.

When completing the form, which must be filled out in the English language (with the exception of foreign LLCs), you should either type or print clearly in black ink all information. The document must be photographed and a permanent record kept by the Department of Commerce. Therefore, if the form is not legible, it will be returned to you unfiled.

Following is a sample filled-in Articles of Organization. We will go step by step through the four articles on the form. **Article I,** the name of the limited liability company, we have already discussed. Be sure to consult our publication, *Naming Your Business and Its Products and Services*, before making your final name selection. This will alert you to the legal pitfalls of a poorly chosen moniker and the potential rewards of an effective and legally defensible commercial name (see the order form in the back of this book for details on this publication). Assuming you have found an available name to your liking, you can fill it in here. Be sure to add after the name one of the following designations: "Limited Liability Company," "L.L.C.," or "L.C."

Article II asks for the purpose of the LLC. Actually, the form already supplies a general purpose clause printed in this space:

The purpose of purposes for which the limited liability company is formed is to engage in any activity within the purposes for which a limited liability company may be formed under the Limited Liability Company Act of Michigan.

This is a wonderfully vague, catch-all purpose. You can add to this general purpose clause, if you like, specifically enumerated

C&S 700 (Rev. (1/96)

MICHIGAN DEPARTMENT OF COMMERCE - CORPORATION AND SECURITIES BUREAU

Date Received			(FOR BUREAU USE ONLY)

Name
Wanda Gold

Address
920 Moose Road

City	State	Zip Code
Dexter, Michigan	48130	

EFFECTIVE DATE:

👈 **Document will be returned to the name and address you enter above** 👉

ARTICLES OF ORGANIZATION
For use by Domestic Limited Liability Companies
(Please read information and instructions on last page)

B						

Pursuant to the provisions of Act 23, Public Acts of 1993, the undersigned execute the following Articles:

ARTICLE I

The name of the limited liability company is: Wanda Gold Enterprises, L.C.

ARTICLE II

The purpose or purposes for which the limited liability company is formed is to engage in any activity within the purposes for which a limited liability company may be formed under the Limited Liability Company Act of Michigan.

ARTICLE III

The duration of the limited liability company is: 30 years

ARTICLE IV

1. The address of the registered office is:

920 Moose Road   Dexter   , Michigan   48130
(Street Address)   (City)   (ZIP Code)

2. The mailing address of the registered office if different than above:

same   , Michigan
(P.O. Box)   (City)   (ZIP Code)

3. The name of the resident agent at the registered office is: Wanda Gold

ARTICLE V (Insert any desired additional provision authorized by the Act; attach additional pages if needed.)

Signed this __7th__ day of __December__ , 19 __96__

By _Wanda Gold_ (Signature)   _Junior Gold_ (Signature)   _____ (Signature)

Wanda Gold
(Type or Print Name)

Junior Gold
(Type or Print Name)

(Type or Print Name)

business purposes you have in mind. We do not recommend this approach, however. In most cases, it is not necessary or even advisable to list the specific types of business activities you will be pursuing.

By making this clause as broad as possible, you allow the future possibility of entering into related or even totally unrelated business endeavors in the future, without the necessity of having to organize a separate business for that specific purpose or to amend the Articles of Organization of your existing business. Although today you are opening an ice cream parlor, tomorrow you may decide to expand your horizons and add—who knows?—a petting zoo! There are legal advantages to general purpose clauses as well, as in the case of an *ultra vires* lawsuit brought by a disgruntled member of the LLC.[2]

Article III concerns the duration of the limited liability company. Unlike a corporation, which typically has a perpetual (unlimited) life, a limited liability company *must* specify a limited period of existence. Although the Michigan statutes do not specify a set period of time for the LLC's duration, an often used term of existence for LLCs is 30 years. Or you may want to list a specific date well into the future, say, December 31, 2080. Such a term of existence would not be unlimited like that of a corporation, but it would obviously exceed the life expectation of most people.

At any rate, the business does not necessarily have to cease to exist after the arrival of the termination date specified in the Articles of Organization. The operating agreement of the LLC can simply specify that the business will be dissolved at the end of the term limit set <u>unless</u> a majority of the members vote to continue the business in its present form.

In the case of LLCs, the death, withdrawal, or bankruptcy of a member can also trigger dissolution of the LLC unless the operating agreement provides otherwise or a majority of the remaining members vote to continue the business, which may involve the admission of one or more new members.

Article IV asks for a mailing address for the registered office of the LLC and the name of the resident agent. What this question really involves is the state of Michigan's way of asking for a legal mailing address for the business and a contact person to whom official mailings, such as annual reports and notice of lawsuits (God forbid!), can be forwarded.

The registered office would ordinarily be the same address as that of the business, and the resident agent would ordinarily be one of the members of the LLC. You can simply fill in the address of the business and your own name in Article IV. A post office mailing address is not acceptable; a street address must be supplied.

---

2   An *ultra vires* act is one in which someone oversteps the bounds of his or her authority, in this particular case, a member or manager who exceeds the authority granted by the Articles of Organization or operating agreement.

Article V provides space to insert any additional provisions, provided that they are authorized by the Michigan Limited Liability Company Act. Article V also notes that additional pages can be attached if needed.

That is the extent of the information required to organize an LLC in Michigan. There is one further step, however. At the bottom of the form is space for the signatures of two or more of the persons who will be members. Underneath the signature lines is space for the signed names to be typed or printed. Since there are three spaces on the form, up to three members can sign. As previously noted, the laws of Michigan do require a minimum of <u>two</u> persons to set up an LLC. Therefore, the Department of Commerce will not accept Articles signed by less than two individuals.

Chapter 3 does provide a way of getting around this two-person requirement, explaining a perfectly legal, although devious, technique of setting up a one-member LLC in Michigan.

Upon your filing of this form, the Department of Commerce will return the original copy to you, indicating its approval. The document is photographed and an optical disk record kept on file by the state of Michigan. Submit completed form to:

Michigan Department of Commerce
Corporation Division
PO Box 30054
Lansing, Michigan 48909

Transferring Assets and Liabilities to Your New Limited Liability Company

When you are ready to start business as a limited liability company, if you are beginning from scratch you will simply turn over the assets or promise to provide assets or services to the LLC in exchange for a membership interest. The actual transfer procedure will be discussed below under "Issuing Certificates of Membership Interest."

If you already have a going business, whether a sole proprietorship, partnership, or corporation, and plan to convert to an LLC, the transfer will be more complicated (particularly in the case of a corporation). Legal counsel is highly advisable when converting from one business form to another, to assure the best arrangement taxwise in your individual circumstances.

If you are beginning with a fresh slate, so to speak, and start off as a limited liability company, you will not have to deal with situations that may trigger taxes when converting from one business structure to another.

Generally, sole proprietorships and partnerships can be converted to limited liability companies tax-free, with few exceptions. Conversions from a corporation to a limited liability company are the most difficult. These will generally involve the liquidation of the corporation, resulting in two levels of tax if the corporation is a C corporation, one level if it is an S corporation. The one exception is the case in which the assets and stock of the corporation have decreased in value instead of increased. Under those circumstances, it may be advantageous taxwise to convert from a corporation to a limited liability company.

In the case of conversions from a sole proprietorship to a limited liability company, the main thing to watch out for is the balance of liabilities and assets transferred from the old business to the new. If the liabilities of the new business exceed the owner's basis in the business assets by a wide margin, this situation may cause the sole proprietor to have a taxable gain at the time of the transfer of the business. Again, plan to consult with a tax adviser knowledgeable in the area of business conversions if you will be changing your business format from that of sole proprietor to a limited liability company. This can prevent future problems with the IRS and assure that your conversion from one business form to another holds no unpleasant tax consequences.

The conversion of a general partnership to an LLC is the least problematic, although there are several technical areas, such as the required method of accounting under the old and new business format, that should also be looked at by a tax practitioner in your individual circumstances. It is also possible to convert a limited partnership to an LLC with relative ease.

Finally, there exists the possibility of converting a corporation (either C or S) to a limited liability company. This type of conversion is the most daunting and filled with pitfalls. First, don't even think of attempting to make this type of switch without professional advice.

One temptation that sometimes arises in the minds of corporate owners who wish to take advantage of certain aspects of the LLC format is that of creating parallel entities. The old corporation is kept intact but a new business entity, an LLC, is set up to essentially run the business. With the case of service businesses, this type of arrangement is especially inviting.

Don't do it. In the first place it is illegal, since you would be siphoning off the corporation's business and drawing on its good will without a formal agreement and appropriate compensation. This type of activity can actually lead to criminal charges against you by the IRS in addition to very hefty tax penalties that would be triggered in such a situation.

There are various legitimate strategies such as the formation of a joint venture and the freezing of the corporation's interest that a knowledgeable tax practitioner can employ in such a situation. As mentioned previously, if the corporation is losing money, the conversion to a limited liability company will be relatively painless. But if the corporation is profitable, the conversion can be challenging as well as expensive, in terms of potential taxes due.

In the case of a new business that wants to start operations as a limited liability company, the procedure for capitalizing the company is relatively easy. Basically, it involves the transfer of the agreed on contributions from the members' pockets to that of the LLC. Michigan law spells out the various forms that member contributions may take. Essentially, a member contribution may consist of any tangible or intangible property or benefit to the company including:

cash, property, services performed, promissory notes, contracts for services to be performed, or other binding obligation to contribute cash or property to perform services (MCLA §450.4301).

A contribution consisting of an obligation to contribute cash or property or services to be performed may be in exchange for a present membership interest or for a future membership interest, including a future profits interest, as provided in the operating agreement. See, however, the warnings in Chapter 4 (page 53) concerning the tax consequences of offering future services to purchase a membership interest in an LLC.

Since a promise by a member to contribute to the limited liability company is not legally enforceable unless set out in writing and signed by the member, we will look at one way of setting up a legally enforceable contribution agreement that each of the members will sign later in this chapter.

Ordering LLC Records Book, Seal, and Member Certificates

The Michigan statutes require that every Michigan limited liability company keep the following records at its registered office:

• a current list of the full name and last known address of each member and manager
• a copy of the Articles or restated Articles of Organization, together with any amendments to the Articles
• copies of the limited liability company's federal, state, and local tax returns and reports, if any, for the 3 most recent years
• copies of any financial statements of the limited liability company for the 3 most recent years
• copies of operating agreements
• copies of records that would enable a member to determine the member's relative shares of the limited liability company's distributions and their relative voting rights

Records

The P. Gaines Co. offers a reasonably priced and attractive **Black Beauty Limited Liability Company Outfit**, *which includes a custom engraved seal, 20 custom printed member certificates, 50 blank sheets of rag content 20-lb. bond Minute Paper as well as a binder with a 7-part index for LLC Articles of Organization and Operating Agreement, Regulations, Members data, Certificates, Transfer Ledger, Minutes, and Financial Reports. Please refer to the back of this book for additional information about this individually customized LLC outfit and an order form.*

Michigan law does not require you to have an LLC seal, but many LLCs do use one. You may be asked for the seal imprint on formal agreements such as the application for the LLC bank accounts, bank loan papers, and lease agreements, although its use, technically speaking, is optional. A seal can be ordered from most stationery stores at a cost of approximately $20 to $25. The LLC outfit advertised in the back of the book also contains an LLC seal. The LLC seal is circular and contains the name of the limited liability company exactly as filed with the Department of Commerce, the name of the state (Michigan), the words "Limited Liability Company SEAL," and the year of organization.

While the Michigan statutes do not require that certificates signed by some or all of the managing members represent the proportional interests of the individual members of LLCs, we do recommend their use as an effective means of organizing the LLC. The certificate is simply a concrete representation of one's capital holdings in the LLC. Rather than share holdings as in the case of corporations, they usually are denominated in unit holdings.

It is standard practice for LLCs to imprint their unit certificates with their seal. Unit certificates for LLCs may be purchased from some of the larger stationery stores. The Black Beauty LLC Outfit offered by the P. Gaines Co. includes 20 Unit Certificates imprinted with the specific name of the LLC and the state of organization.

Preorganization Subscription Agreement

If you form a one-person LLC following the procedure outlined in Chapter 3, then a subscription agreement will not be necessary, of course. If other members will be involved in setting up the limited liability company as well, then it is a good idea to have each of you sign a "preorganization subscription agreement." A sample filled-in form appears on the following page.

As noted on page 66 above, a promise by a member to contribute to the limited liability company is not legally enforceable unless set out in writing and signed by the member. By using a preorganization subscription agreement form, you will have an agreement that is legally binding in the state of Michigan.

Once Articles of Organization are filed with the Department of Commerce, all subscribers for ownership interests shall be deemed to be members of the LLC. Subscriptions for unit interests are normally to be paid following the first organizational meeting.

As previously noted, a contribution consisting of an obligation to contribute cash or property or services to be performed (such as a promissory note) may be in exchange for a present membership interest or for a future membership interest, including a future profits interest, as provided in the operating agreement.

In the case of default, the LLC may proceed to collect the amount due in the

PREORGANIZATION SUBSCRIPTION AGREEMENT

We, the undersigned, severally subscribe to the number of units set opposite our respective names of capital of a proposed limited liability company, to be known as **WANDA GOLD ENTERPRISES, L.C.** or by any other name that the members may select, and to be organized in the State of Michigan. We agree to pay the sum of $ **20.00** per each unit subscribed.

This subscription shall not be binding on the undersigned unless subscriptions in the aggregate amount of $ **20,000.00** for units of said limited liability company have been procured on or before the **7th** day of **December**, 19 **96**.

All subscriptions hereto shall be payable at such time or times as the members of said limited liability company may determine and shall be paid in cash, except as hereinafter indicated. (If any of the subscriptions are to be paid by transferring property or offering services to the limited liability company, a description of the property and/or services shall be attached hereto.)

Date	Name and Address	Number of Units	Amount Subscribed
11-29-96	Wanda Gold 920 Moose Road Dexter, Michigan 48130	500	$10,000.00
11-30-96	Junior Gold 912 Vintus Blvd Dexter, Michigan 48130	(250)	$5,000.00
11/1/96	GIESELA GOLD 814 PERSIMMON LANE SALINE, MICHIGAN 48196	250	$5,000.00

68

same manner as any debt. It may also rescind the subscription and sue the defaulter for breach of contract. See Appendix E for a blank copy of this agreement which you can adopt for your own LLC. If you have more member-subscribers than you can fit on one sheet, you can make as many additional copies of this form as necessary.

Preparing the Operating Agreement

You are now ready to prepare the operating agreement for your limited liability company, which may contain any provision for the regulation or management of the affairs of the limited liability company and the conduct of its business that is not inconsistent with law or the Articles of Organization.Some states allow the operating agrement of an LLC to be oral. Michigan law specifies that it <u>must</u> be in writing.

The initial operating agreement of a Michigan limited liability company shall be adopted by unanimous vote of the members. Amendment of the operating agreement may be made by majority vote of the members, unless the operating agreement provides otherwise.

We provide in Appendix B in the back of this book an operating agreement which you can use as is or modify to suit yourself. We have designed this operating agreement to conform to the requirements of the Michigan laws regulating the operation of limited liability companies in this state. If you are having an attorney prepare your limited liability company organization, you might want to use the operating agreement in the back of the book, with changes, as needed. You will pay dearly if he or she draws up a customized operating agreement from scratch.

Organizational Meeting of Members

After the limited liability company has been organized and the Articles of Organization filed with the Department of Commerce and returned to you approved, it is a good idea to have a meeting of the members. We include sample minutes of this meeting in Appendix C to provide a framework for the major decisions that need to be made at this point. The meeting should be advised that the Articles of Organization have been filed and approved. The operating agreement should also be read point by point, discussed, and approved.

If a preorganization subscription agreement has been used, it should be read, and the contributions to which each member has committed should be turned over or signed over to the limited liability company. In the case of the promise of future contributions, these can be read and acknowledged by all the members.

If you are transferring the assets and liabilities of a going business to the limited liability company in exchange for a membership interest, then the two resolutions dealing with the transfer need to be filled out. If you are the sole owner of a proprietorship and are transferring this business to the limited liability company, a "Bill of Sale Agreement" should be executed (see Appendix E for a model of this form). The date of the offer of transfer of business, which details the assets and liabilities of the business being transferred, and the fair market value of the business should be indicated in the appropriate blanks.

Issues such as whether the limited liability company will be member-managed or manager-managed should have already been discussed and decided on, but you may need to work out some of the fine tuning of this matter at this time.

How key duties such as those involving the finances and the administrative aspects of the business will be performed needs to be decided as well, if not already spelled out. Perhaps one member will assume responsibility for the role of treasurer and another for secretary for a set period of time, such as one year, or the members will agree upon sharing these tasks on some sort of rotating basis.

At this meeting, you will also probably want to:

• approve the LLC seal and unit certificates
• establish a tax year for the business
• decide on a bank or banks where the company will maintain its accounts
• choose either a cash or accrual method of accounting

When a resolution concerning the LLC seal and unit certificate has been read and passed, the acting secretary should make an impression of the seal in the right-hand margin of the minutes.

Regarding the selection of a tax year, LLCs, like partnerships, ordinarily must choose a tax year that is the same as 50 percent or more of its members. In most cases, this will mean a tax year that corresponds with the calendar year, running from January 1 to December 31.

However, you also have the option of having your fiscal year be another 12-month period ending on the last day of September, October, or November (September 1 to October 30, for example).

The establishment of a tax year entails various tax and accounting questions. There are also certain additional limitations that the IRS may impose on your election. Therefore, you will want to consult a tax adviser about this issue if you have reason to choose a tax year other than the calendar year.

The choice of a bank or banks for business accounts should be made. If you wish more than one member to endorse checks, you should insert a separate resolution to this effect.

The choice of the method of accounting that the business will follow must be made. A business using the cash method of accounting deducts expenses when paid and records income when received. By contrast, under the accrual method a business reports expenses when incurred, regardless of when actually paid, and income when a sale is made, regardless of when the payment for the sale is received. There are advantages and disadvantages to each type of accounting method, depending on individual business situations. Some businesses are **required** by the IRS to use the accrual method, such as businesses with inventory and those classified as "syndicates" (enterprises which allot more than 35 percent of their losses to members who are not active participants in the running of the business). Again, the question of accounting method appropriate to your individual LLC is one best answered by an accountant.

If you intend to have company benefit plans, such as a "Medical Care Reimbursement Plan," these should be adopted at this meeting as well. With this type of plan, the business will pay the medical expenses of the employees and their dependents, either on a limited or an unlimited basis (one type of model plan, included in Appendix E, allows you to set a dollar ceiling on the benefits paid per year or to have no ceiling). Be sure to work with your tax adviser in setting up such a model plan. Keep in mind that the benefits paid by such plans will ordinarily be taxable to the recipient in the year of receipt.

As previously pointed out, it is important to have a company records book, whether a 3-ring binder or the Black Beauty LLC Outfit which The P. Gaines Co. sells. Michigan law requires key records to be kept, as enumerated on page 66 above. In this records book will be kept copies of the Articles of Organization, the operating agreement, a sample copy of the LLC's unit certificate, a copy of the bank depository form, and other applicable forms, a stub or photocopy of the unit certificates issued showing the member contributions, minutes of meetings, a listing of member names and addresses, as well as tax returns and financial reports for the three most recent years.

In the sample operating agreement in Appendix B, we have included a section that makes the calling of meetings for members and their actual holding as flexible and open-ended as possible. A phone conference, for example, may constitute a meeting. Since your time as a business owner is valuable, there is certainly no reason to waste it with a lot of unnecessary formalities. One reason to opt for an LLC as a way of doing business is to take advantage of its informality in the area of member meetings and not set up a rigid schedule of required quarterly meetings, for example.

But, perhaps you favor highly structured activities (your friends refer to you behind your back as the "retentive type.") It is good to know that you also have the option of having a meeting of members at 2:00 in the afternoon on the third Tuesday of each month, if desired.

71

Special Meetings

Other than the initial meeting(s) of the members necessary to organize the LLC, you do not have to hold regularly scheduled meetings at a set time, like corporations. There will be occasions, of course, when a meeting will need to be called. Your LLC members will want to call a special meeting in situations such as these, for example:

• to amend the LLC Articles of Organization
• to amend the operating agreement, say, when a new member is admitted or a current member leaves
• to approve or change benefit plans, for instance, to set up or amend a medical reimbursement plan or a pension plan
• to initiate a lawsuit or answer a lawsuit brought against the LLC
• to make major financial decisions, such as those involved in buying or selling real estate or other property

It is a good idea to specify in the operating agreement the basic procedure for notifying members of meetings and to stick to it. In the sample operating agreement in Appendix B, we specify advance notice of a special meeting, to be given by mail, fax, or phone, with at least 10 days' notice. In the event of some development requiring immediate action, we specify a procedure whereby a written notice of the action can be circulated to all the members, for their signatures.

Issuing Certificates of Membership Interest

Once the organizational meeting of the members concludes, certificates can now be issued to represent units of membership interest. As we have seen, certificates can be issued in exchange for cash, real property (including the assets of a going business), or services.

One issue that you need to be aware of is the possibility that issuance of membership interest in an LLC may be classed as a "security" under federal and state laws. First, if your LLC will be member managed, you are off the hook. You don't need to worry about security laws, since your membership interests will not be classified as "securities."

LLCs which will be partly or wholly managed by non-members are a different kettle of fish. Depending on the size of the business, you may or may not have to register with the federal and state securities offices and pay a registration fee. If the membership of your LLC consists of 35 or fewer members and your business will not be engaged in interstate commerce, you can likely claim an exemption from securities registration. To be on the safe side, any LLC that is not wholly member-managed should work with a legal adviser on this matter. Certain safeguards, such as specific wording positioned on your certificates of membership interest, can be set in place by a knowledgeable practitioner. [3]

Each certificate can represent any number of units of membership interest, the number of units to be indicated in the box in the upper right-hand corner of the certificate. A sample certificate appears on the next page. Instructions for filling it out follow hereafter.

Instructions for Filling Out Certificates

First, fill out the stub portion of the certificates, which is either attached directly to the certificates or separate. The stubs are attached to the certificates in this book.

First, detach the stub from the certificate and fill it out as follows. Two of the three headings on the stub say "To Be Filled In At Time of Issue"—fill these sections in now. The third section, in the middle of the stub, says "To Be Filled In At Time of Transfer." This section is filled in only if and when the certificate is transferred to a new owner.

On the left side of the stub, fill in the certificate number. You will simply number, in sequence, each certificate to be issued, 1,2,3., etc. (If you have more members than the number of certificates in this book, you will need to purchase additional certificates, of course.) Be sure that the number on the stub matches the corresponding number on the face of the certificate. The stub numbered 1 will be the company record of the certificate numbered 1, issued to a particular member, and so on.

Moving down the stub, next indicate the number of units purchased by that individual and the name of the person to whom issued and fill in the date on the bottom line of the stub.

The number of units you might think of as simply a bookkeeping device that enables you to indicate the proportion of ownership that each member holds in the limited liability company. If you have only two member-owners, for instance, and each has a 50 percent ownership interest in the company, it doesn't matter whether you show that equal proportion with, say, each of them owning 100 units a piece, or 500 units a piece, or 10,000 units a piece. In each case, each member holds half of the total ownership units. Just pick an arbitrary number of units to represent 100 percent ownership of the company and then carve up pieces of that unit-pie among the different members according to their percentage of ownership.

Leave the middle section, as noted, blank. This is only used in case of transfer of the certificate to a new owner.

On the right side of the stub, you again fill in the certificate number and the date of issuance. You then have the member sign on

---

[3] You can reach the Michigan Securities Division by telephone at (517) 334-6200; the mailing address is PO Box 30222, Lansing, Michigan 48909.

Certificate Number ___1___

Units ___500___

WANDA GOLD ENTERPRISES, L.C.

A LIMITED LIABILITY COMPANY ORGANIZED UNDER THE LAWS OF THE STATE OF MICHIGAN

This Certifies That ___Wanda Gold___ is a member of the above named Limited Liability Company and is the owner of ___500___ Units of the said company. He/she is entitled to the full rights and privileges of such membership, subject to the restrictions in the Articles of Organization and Operating Agreement for the Limited Liability Company.

The membership interest represented by this Certificate is subject to restrictions on transfer, a copy of which is available free of charge upon request from an officer of the LLC at the following address:

___920 Moose Road, Dexter, Michigan 48130___

In Witness Whereof, the said Limited Liability Company has caused this Certificate to be signed by its duly authorized Member(s)/Manager(s) and to be sealed with the seal of the Limited Liability Company.

Date ___12/7/96___   *Wanda Gold*   *Jennifer Gold*

the bottom line as an acknowledgment of receipt.

On the certificate proper, indicate the certificate number in the upper left-hand corner and the number of units represented by the certificate in the upper right-hand corner. Fill in the name of the limited liability company in the large center blank.

In the body of the certificate, you may simply fill in the blanks for the owner's name and number of units. The next blank is used to indicate the business address of the LLC.

The date of issuance should also be shown in the place provided at the bottom left of the certificate. There is also space at the bottom of the certificate to type in the name(s) of the company officer(s) after each has signed in the appropriate space.

Finally, an impression of the company seal may be made at the bottom of the certificate, in the center.

Each member is given a completed certificate in exchange for cash or other tangible property or the promise of services to be performed (see the warning about the taxability of promised services on page 53, however). Ownership interests in exchange for cash should be paid for by personal check so that the member will have proof of payment. It is recommended that receipt for cash payment also be issued by the LLC,
showing the amount of money received, the check number, the name of the member and the number of units purchased, the name of the limited liability company, and the name of the treasurer, as well as the treasurer's signature.

A duplicate copy of each member's receipt should be kept in the certificates section of the company records book. In regard to certificates issued in exchange for other tangible property (which may consist of part or all the assets of a going business), a copy of a signed and dated bill of sale[4] will provide documentation of this transaction.

Employer Identification Number

As soon as possible after filing the Articles of Organization and selecting a tax year for your LLC, you should apply to the IRS for an Employer Identification Number (EIN). You may already have an EIN if you are in business as a sole proprietor or other business entity. This one won't work, however. You will be required to obtain a new EIN as an LLC. The one exception is the conversion of a partnership to an LLC, which does not require a new EIN.

The form to file is an SS-4, Application for Employer Identification Number. You can phone your local IRS office and request

---

4   See Appendix E for a copy of a Bill of Sale agreement that you may use, with modifications appropriate to the circumstances, for these types of transfers.

an SS-4 by mail or pick one up in person. (See the phone directory in the back of this book for a national number you can call for IRS forms.) It will usually take 3 to 6 weeks after applying to receive your number.

If any forms, such as your application for a bank account, ask for the EIN before it arrives, you can put down "number applied for," with the understanding that you will notify the appropriate authorities immediately upon receipt.

Filing an Assumed Name and Other Changes

There is one more procedure that may or may not apply to your newly formed LLC. Say you organize your video business under the name of Megamasters of the Seventh Ray of Ocham Video Store. In the course of doing business—answering the phone, talking to potential customers, and so on—you find yourself shortening the name to Megamasters Video. Advertisements that you run for your business also use this shortened form of the name. When you order a new batch of business stationery, you decide to go with the short form of the name as well.

Since you are not using the exact legal name registered with the state of Michigan in your LLC Articles of Organization, you must file this "fictitious name" with the Department of Commerce. Request a copy of the Certificate of Assumed Name from the Department of Commerce and submit it with a $10 fee payment. The registration is good for 5 years (such a bargain!). It may be renewed within 90 days of expiration. Your business will automatically be notified of the impending expiration.

Whenever the name under which you do business is different in some way from the one you originally filed when you submitted your Articles of Organization, you must follow this procedure. If you operate under the exact name, as filed, then it is, of course, not necessary to file an assumed name application.

You may also need at some point to make other changes in your LLC, such as amending its Articles of Organization, changing the name of your business because of a trademark conflict[5] or a poorly chosen moniker that turns customers off, or changing the LLC's registered office or registered agent. Contact the Michigan Department of Commerce for the filing procedure and the fee schedule whenever it is necessary to make these or other changes in your LLC.

---

5   See above, pages 58-60, on ways to avoid the serious problem of trademark or trade name infringement.

Chapter 6. THE MICHIGAN PROFESSIONAL LIMITED LIABILITY COMPANY

The Michigan law authorizing limited liability companies in this state allows for LLCs to be organized for any lawful purpose, including providing professional services. The actual organizational process to set up an LLC in Michigan is so simple that it should take no more than 5 minutes to fill out the necessary form. The form requires only the name, address, specified number of years the company will be in existence (usually 30), and the signature of the filer. A filing fee of $50 must accompany the completed form.

The important issue, of course, is the decision on whether it is more advantageous to organize your professional service as a corporation or as an LLC. Some states do not yet allow all professionals to set up LLCs. Illinois, for example, does not allow the practice of law by LLCs at this time. Michigan has no limitation on any professional groups setting up LLCs in the state.

One other word of caution: two states at present do not have LLC legislation in place. If you are considering setting up a multistate professional practice as an LLC, you will probably not have liability protection for your members in those two states— Hawaii and Vermont. It is simply a matter of time before these two states pass LLC laws, but right now they remain devoid of LLC legal guidelines. If your professional practice does not extend to these two states, this issue will have no bearing on you.

Liability Issues

Neither LLCs nor corporations shield the professional practitioner from liability for his professional actions, of course. Both the corporation and the LLC forms may provide some protection from liability due to actions of member-associates, however.

Thus, both corporate and LLC statutes may provide explicit or implicit protection from what is termed "vicarious liability." If so, an "innocent" member who did not commit, and did not have the duty to supervise or control the act leading to professional liability would not be liable for damages. In this respect, corporations and LLCs are on equal footing, shielding their members from vicarious liability in some cases. In some states, this liability shield is not operable in the case of attorneys who are shareholders in professional corporations or who are members of a professional LLC.[1]

Cost of Organization

In some states, the LLC registration fees are substantially higher than the organizational fees for other types of business entities. In such cases, the organizational costs may be prohibitive. In Illinois, for example, LLCs pay an initial registration fee of $500, five times the cost of organizing a corporation, plus an annual filing fee of $300 (most corporations pay an annual filing fee of $40). In Michigan, by contrast, the fee is not a deciding factor, since both the corporate and LLC organizational costs are the same very low fee of $50.

Choice of State

In the case of multistate professional practices, it is necessary to consider under which state's statute to organize the LLC. Such a situation will necessitate a close comparison of the differences in state laws governing such key issues as ease of organization, the actual operation of an LLC, governance, mergers, and dissolution. States can differ substantially in certain of these points, making it more advantageous to organize in certain states than in others.

State Taxation

It is important to review the manner in which an LLC is taxed in your state. Many states impose no tax on the LLC entity itself, in which case the LLC would provide an advantage over a professional corporation subject to an entity tax. In other states, such as Texas and Florida, substantial entity-level taxes are imposed, thus making the LLC form less attractive to professionals in those states. In the case of Michigan, an LLC pays the same entity tax as a corporation, 2.3 percent of its tax basis, but this tax does not apply to businesses below a certain size (only businesses whose annual gross receipts exceed $250 thousand

---

1   Notably, Illinois, Delaware, Wisconsin, Ohio, Georgia, Indiana, and Nebraska have all had court cases which did not allow innocent shareholders to escape liability arising from malpractice by associates. In discussing the liability of members of a Michigan professional LLC, secton 450.4905 of the law states simply: "The limited liability company shall be liable up to the full value of its property for any negligent or wrongful acts or misconduct committed by any of its members, managers, employees, or agents while they are engaged on behalf of the company in the rendering of professional services."

must file a Michigan state tax return and pay the tax).

Conversion of an Existing Professional Practice to an LLC

There are various tax ramifications for existing professional associations converting to LLCs. In the case of a partnership converting to an LLC, the conversion is generally tax-free. By contrast, a firm organized as a professional corporation (without S status) will often trigger taxes for the individual shareholders and most likely for the corporation as well when converting to an LLC. These types of situations and the taxes involved should be explored with a competent legal adviser.

Authorized Form

The form to file with the Michigan Department of Commerce in order to organize your professional practice as an LLC is Form 701. A blank copy of this form is found in Appendix E in the back of this book. On the following two pages appears a sample filled-in form.

Article I: Name
In completing the Articles of Organization form, the first item, the LLC name, is subject to the provisions of Article 9 of the Michigan Limited Liability Company Act which specifies that:

The name of the limited liability company shall contain the words "professional limited liability company" or the abbreviation "P.L.L.C." or "P.L.C."

Article II: Specific Purpose
The second item on the form asks the preparer to fill in the specific professional service or services that the limited liability company will render. 'Professional service' means a type of personal service to the public that requires as a precondition to rendering of the service the obtaining of a license or other legal authorization (§450.4902). In Michigan, professional service includes, but is not limited to, services rendered by certified or other public accountants, chiropractors, dentists, optometrists, veterinarians, osteopaths, physicians and surgeons, doctors of medicine, doctors of dentistry, podiatrists, chiropodists, architects, professional engineers, land surveyors, and attorneys.

Article III: Duration
The preparer of the form is asked to specify a particular duration of the LLC. The standard period is 30 years. As previously noted, you don't have to dissolve the company at that point. The members at the end of the 30 years (or whatever period you specify) will simply have to take a vote as to whether to continue the business.

MICHIGAN DEPARTMENT OF COMMERCE - CORPORATION AND SECURITIES BUREAU

Date Received			(FOR BUREAU USE ONLY)

Name	Wanda Gold		
Address	920 Moose Road		
City	Dexter, Michigan	State	Zip Code 48130

EFFECTIVE DATE:

☜ Document will be returned to the name and address you enter above ☞

L	C	—			

ARTICLES OF ORGANIZATION
For use by Domestic Professional Service Limited Liability Companies
(Please read information and instructions on last page)

Pursuant to the provisions of Act 23, Public Acts of 1993, the undersigned execute the following Articles:

ARTICLE I

The name of the professional limited liability company is:
Buena Vista Veterinary Services, P.L.C.

ARTICLE II

The limited liability company is organized for the sole and specific purpose of rendering the following professional service(s):
The practice of veterinary medicine in all its forms

ARTICLE III

The duration of the limited liability company is: _____ 30 years _____

ARTICLE IV

1. The address of the registered office is:
920 Moose Road   Dexter   , Michigan   48130
(Street Address)   (City)   (ZIP Code)

2. The mailing address of the registered office if different than above:
same   , Michigan _____
(P.O. Box)   (City)   (ZIP Code)

3. The name of the resident agent at the registered office is: _____ Wanda Gold _____

80

ARTICLE V

All members will be duly licensed or otherwise legally authorized to render one or more of the professional service(s) for which this limited liability company is organized except as otherwise provided in Section 904(2) of this Act or prohibited by law.

Signed this _____ 19th _____ day of _____ January _____, 19 _____ 1997 _____

_____
(Signature)

_____
Wanda Gold, D.V.M.
(Type or Print Name)

_____
(Signature)

_____
(Type or Print Name)

_____
(Signature)

_____
Allen Park, D.V.M.
(Type or Print Name)

_____
(Signature)

_____
(Type or Print Name)

Article IV: Registered Office and Resident Agent

A Michigan street address and mailing address, if different from the street address, as well as the name of a contact person must be provided. This information is needed in order to give the state of Michigan a legal contact and address for any mailings related to the LLC, whether tax forms or legal notifications, as in the case of a lawsuit filed against the company.

Article V: Signature

By signing the form, the members of the LLC testify to the validity of the statement preprinted on the form at this point:

All members will be duly licensed or otherwise legally authorized to render one or more of the professional service(s) for which this limited liability company is organized except as otherwise provided in Section 904(2) of this Act or prohibited by law.

A minimum of two licensed persons must sign the form in order to establish a professional limited liability company under Michigan law.[2]

Limit on Business Activities

As already noted, the member/employees of your professional LLC cannot engage in any business other than rendering those professional services for which they are licensed, as specifically noted in the Articles of Organization. Of course, clerical and secretarial employees are exceptions to this rule. Your professional LLC may employ these types of workers to render services of a nonprofessional nature (§450.4905).

Your professional LLC is permitted to own stocks, bonds, mortgages, real estate, and other types of real or personal property necessary for the rendering of professional services. In most cases, your professional LLC can own any type of investment without limitation but be sure to check with your tax adviser on this point in your particular situation. If, for example, your professional LLC is buying up huge tracts of raw land for speculative purposes, this activity may very well be overstepping the bounds of what is legally permissible.

Fringe Benefits

We have already looked at the main fringe benefits available to limited liability companies. These will be the same for professional LLCs, chief among which is the right to set up a retirement plan and the right to deduct a portion of medical insurance premiums. See pages 54-57 for a thorough discussion of these two areas.

---

2   See, however, Chapter 3 for a way around the two-person requirement for the single person interested in forming an LLC. The same procedure may be followed for a single-member professional limited liability company.

Tax Treatment

The tax treatment of LLCs is examined in detail in Chapter 4, "Taxes and the Michigan Limited Liability Company." On the federal level, all profits (or losses) of the professional LLC will pass through to the individual members and will be taxed (or deducted) at their individual rates. On the state level, an entity tax of 2.3 percent of income may be due if the gross receipts of the business exceed $250 thousand for tax year 1996.

Annual Report and Filing Fee

Each year, a professional limited liability company must file with the state of Michigan by February 15 an annual report, with a $50 filing fee. The report must list the names and addresses of all members and managers and certify that all members and managers are licensed or otherwise duly authorized to render within the state the same professional services that the company was formed to render.

The annual report form should be mailed to you automatically each year at the registered office address provided in the Articles of Organization. If you do not receive it by January 15, notify the Michigan Department of Commerce.

Mergers

A professional LLC may merge only with another LLC whose members and managers are licensed persons (§450.4910).

Restrictions on Membership Interests

If a member or manager of a professional limited liability company becomes legally disqualified to render the professional service rendered by the company, he or she shall sever within a reasonable period all employment with and financial interests in the company. A company's failure to require compliance with this requirement constitutes a ground for the forfeiture of its Articles of Organization and its dissolution (§450.4906).

A membership interest in a professional LLC shall not be sold or transferred except:

(1) to a person who is eligible to be a member of the company; **or**
(2) to the personal representative or estate of a deceased or legally incompetent member.

The personal representative or estate of the member may continue to hold a membership interest for a reasonable period but shall not be authorized to participate in any decisions concerning the rendering of professional service (§450.4908).

The Articles of Organization or an operating agreement of a professional LLC may provide specifically for additional restrictions on the transfer of membership interests.

APPENDIX A

Articles of Organization for Michigan Domestic Limited Liability Companies (Form 700)

MICHIGAN DEPARTMENT OF COMMERCE - CORPORATION AND SECURITIES BUREAU

Date Received			(FOR BUREAU USE ONLY)

Name

Address

City   State   Zip Code

EFFECTIVE DATE:

↳ Document will be returned to the name and address you enter above ↲

ARTICLES OF ORGANIZATION
For use by Domestic Limited Liability Companies
(Please read information and instructions on last page)

B ☐ ☐ ☐ ☐ ☐ ☐ ☐

Pursuant to the provisions of Act 23, Public Acts of 1993, the undersigned execute the following Articles:

ARTICLE I

The name of the limited liability company is: _____

ARTICLE II

The purpose or purposes for which the limited liability company is formed is to engage in any activity within the purposes for which a limited liability company may be formed under the Limited Liability Company Act of Michigan.

ARTICLE III

The duration of the limited liability company is: _____

ARTICLE IV

1. The address of the registered office is:

_____ , Michigan _____
(Street Address)   (City)   (ZIP Code)

2. The mailing address of the registered office if different than above:

_____ , Michigan _____
(P.O. Box)   (City)   (ZIP Code)

3. The name of the resident agent at the registered office is: _____

ARTICLE V (Insert any desired additional provision authorized by the Act; attach additional pages if needed.)

Signed this _____ day of _____ , 19 _____

By _____   _____   _____
(Signature)   (Signature)   (Signature)

_____   _____   _____
(Type or Print Name)   (Type or Print Name)   (Type or Print Name)

Name of Person or Organization Remitting Fees:	Preparer's Name and Business Telephone Number:
_____	_____
_____	( ) _____

INFORMATION AND INSTRUCTIONS

1. The articles of organization cannot be filed until this form, or a comparable document, is submitted.

2. Submit one original of this document. Upon filing, the document will be added to the records of the Corporation and Securities Bureau. The original will be returned to the address you enter in the box on the front as evidence of filing.

   Since this document will be maintained on optical disc media, it is important that the filing be legible. Documents with poor black and white contrast, or otherwise illegible, will be rejected.

3. This document is to be used pursuant to the provisions of Act 23, P.A. of 1993, by two or more persons for the purpose of forming a domestic limited liability company. **Use form 701 if the Limited Liability Company will be providing a personal service for which a license or legal authorization is required pursuant to Article 9 of the Act.**

4. Article I - The name of a domestic limited liability company is required to contain one of the following words or abbreviations: "Limited Liability Company", "L.L.C.", or "L.C."

5. Article II - Under section 203(b) of the Act, it is sufficient to state substantially, alone or with specifically enumerated purposes, that the limited liability company is formed to engage in any activity within the purposes for which a limited liability company may be formed under the Act.

6. Article III - The term of existence of the limited liability company must be reflected as a specific date, a number of years, or perpetual.

7. Article IV - A post office box may not be designated as the address of the registered office.

8. Article V - Section 401 of the Act specifically states the business shall be managed by members unless the articles of organization state the business will be managed by managers. If the limited liability company is to be managed by managers instead of by members, insert a statement to that effect in Article V.

9. This document is effective on the date endorsed "Filed" by the Bureau. A later effective date, no more than 90 days after the date of delivery, may be stated as an additional article.

10. The articles must be signed in ink by two or more of the persons who will be members. Names of person signing shall be stated beneath their signatures.

11. If more space is needed, attach additional pages. All pages should be numbered.

12. **FEES:** Make remittance payable to the State of Michigan. Include limited liability company name on check or money order. **Nonrefundable filing fee** **$50.00**

13. Mail form and fee to:

    Michigan Department of Commerce
    Corporation and Securities Bureau
    Corporation Division
    P.O. Box 30054
    Lansing, MI 48909-7554

    The office is located at:

    6546 Mercantile Way
    Lansing, MI 48910
    (517) 334-6302

APPENDIX B

Operating Agreement

OPERATING AGREEMENT FOR MEMBER-MANAGED MICHIGAN LIMITED LIABILITY COMPANY

Article I
Company Organization

(1) *Initial Date.* This limited liability company Agreement is first made on _____ (date) by _____ (name of company). This Agreement is hereby adopted by the persons who on the above named date are members of the company. The signatures of the members which attest to their adoption of this Agreement appear at the end of this document.

(2) *Formation.* The members formed this limited liability company (LLC) by filing Articles of Organization with the Michigan Department of Commerce on _____ (date). A copy of this filed Form 700 has been placed in the LLC records book.

(3) *Name.* The name of this LLC filed with the Michigan Department of Commerce is such as is stated above. The company may choose, however, to do business under a fictitious name by filing a Certificate of Assumed Name with the Michigan Department of Commerce.

(4) *Registered Office and Agent.* The location of the registered office of this LLC shall be:
_____.
The company's registered agent at such address shall be: _____.
If the registered office or the registered agent change, it will not be necessary to amend this provision of the operating agreement to reflect this change. Instead, the change(s) will need to be filed with the Michigan Department of Commerce.

(5) *Term.* The duration of this company shall be _____ years, unless dissolved by the members according to the procedures discussed below under "Dissolution" or otherwise terminated by law.

(6) *Business Purpose.* This LLC may engage in any and all business activities permitted companies organized under the Michigan Limited Liability Company Act. In light of this broad business purpose allowed LLCs formed under this act, the founding members of this LLC may state the *specific* business purposes and activities they intend to pursue in the following space: _____
_____

Article II
Membership

(1) *Signature Requirement.* Any person desiring to become a member of this LLC must indicate formal acceptance of this Agreement by affixing his or her signature.

(2) *Governance.* This company will be managed exclusively by its members.

(3) *Authority of Members.* The members as a group have sole authority to manage the company. The members acting as a group may designate one or more individual members to make contracts or enter into other types of transactions or commitments on behalf of the company. Unless delegated by the group to do so, no individual member has the authority to act as the agent of the company.

(4) *Acts of Members.* An act of the members consists of a majority vote of the membership units at a meeting, scheduled according to the requirement enumerated in section 8 of Article II, or by written action without a meeting, as provided in section 8 of Article II.

(5) *Nonliability of Members.* To the full extent permitted by the Michigan Limited Liability Company Act, no member of an LLC in this state shall be personally liable for the debts or other liabilities of the LLC. All members, furthermore, are released from liability for damages on account of any act, omission, or conduct in the member's managerial role. According to the Michigan statutes (§450.4407), members will **not** be released from liability for breach of duty, however, in the following 3 instances: (a) the receipt of a financial benefit to which the member is not entitled; (b) the making of an unlawful distribution; (c) a knowing violation of law.

(6) *Reimbursement.* The LLC shall reimburse the members for start-up expenses paid by the members to organize the company, as well as for out-of-pocket expenses incurred by the members in managing the company.

(7) *Compensation.* Members will not be paid by the company for performing duties conferred by their membership interests, including management of the LLC. Members who also serve in other capacities as officers, employees, or agents of the company will be compensated for their services. Most businesses, including LLCs, require a minimum of two officer functions, that of the chief executive officer and the chief financial officer, which traditionally are paid positions.

(8) *Member Meetings.* The LLC shall not hold regularly scheduled member meetings. Any member, however, may call a meeting by communicating to all the other members, by writing, phone, fax, or other form of electronic communication, the intention to hold a meeting at a reasonable time and place.

Unless all the members can attend the meeting, it will be postponed unless those who cannot attend grant their permission in writing for the holding of the meeting without them. Advance notice need not be given of the business to be discussed at the meeting—any topic may be discussed and any business transacted.

Written minutes of the meeting shall be made by one of the members or by another designated person. The minutes shall cover any proposals discussed, votes taken, and actions declined or approved. A copy of the minutes of the meeting shall be kept in the LLC records book.

Any action that may be taken at a meeting may be taken without a meeting by unanimous consent of all the members in writing.

(9) *Membership Certificates.* This LLC shall issue certificates representing membership interests in the company. Each certificate shall state: the name of the LLC; the name of the member; that the member is entitled to the full rights and privileges of such membership, subject to any restrictions in the Articles of Organization and this Operating Agreement.

Each membership certificate shall be consecutively numbered and shall show the number of membership units represented by the certificate (discussed below). Each certificate shall be signed by one or more officers of the LLC and shall be imprinted with the company seal.

The certificate shall state on its front that the membership interest represented by the certificate is subject to restrictions on transfer under the Articles of Organization and/or the provisions of this Operating Agreement. The address of the LLC where a copy of these transfer restrictions may be obtained shall be stated on the face of the certificate as well.

The LLC shall maintain a list in its records book of the names and addresses of all persons to whom certificates have been issued. In addition, the LLC shall record the date of issuance of each certificate and the date of any cancellations or transfers of membership certificates.

(10) *Calculation of Membership Interests.* Each member's percentage interest in the LLC shall be computed by dividing the total value of the member's capital contributions by the total value of all the members' capital contributions. For example, in the case of Mystique, L.L.C., a Michigan limited liability company, two of the four members contribute $10,000 in cash to the startup business; the other two members contribute $30,000 each in cash. The two members contributing $10,000 would have a 12.5% membership interest ($10,000 divided by $80,000). The two members contributing $30,000 would have a 37.5% membership interest ($30,000 divided by $80,000).

The respective percentages of member interests shall be expressed on the membership certificates in terms of the number of membership units, to be shown in the upper right hand corner of the certificate. The number of units shown can simply be the same as the percentage interest of the member, or, to avoid fractional units, it can be shown as a multiple of 10. In our example, the members contributing $10,000 would be issued membership certificates representing 125 units each, whereas the $30,000 contributors would receive certificates representing 375 units. The whole pie (100% of membership interests) would be represented by 1000 units in this particular example.

(11) *Membership Voting.* Except as may otherwise be required by the Articles of Organization, other provisions of this Operating Agreement, or the laws of Michigan, each member shall vote on any matter submitted to the membership in proportion to the member's percentage interest in the LLC. In the above example, the $30,000 contributors would therefore possess 3 votes for each single vote of the $10,000 contributors.

In this Operating Agreement, the phrase "majority of members" means a number of members whose combined percentage of membership interests in this LLC represent more than 50% of the total percentage of membership interests. In our example, the two $30,000 contributors would represent a majority of members (representing 75% of combined membership interests) or one $30,000 contributor and two $10,000 contributors would comprise a majority of members (representing 72.5% of total membership interests). By contrast, one $10,000 contributor and one $30,000 contributor would <u>not</u> comprise a majority of members, since their combined membership interests would total exactly 50%.

Article III
Tax and Other Financial Matters

(1) *Tax Treatment of LLC.* The members agree that this LLC will be taxed as a partnership for federal and Michigan state tax purposes. All provisions of this Agreement and the company's Articles of Organization are designed to support this claim of partnership tax status. The members do not consider each other partners or joint venturers for any purpose other than that of establishing partnership tax status.

(2) *Tax Year.* The tax year of the LLC shall be the calendar year unless all the members agree to a different tax year, namely that stated hereafter: _____. (If the company adopts a different tax year than the calendar year, it must be one that is legally allowable; the proper state and federal forms must be filed, furthermore.) This tax year may be changed with the approval of all the members and the filing of the appropriate federal and state tax forms.

(3) *Accounting Method.* This LLC shall use the _____ method of accounting.

(4) *Bank Accounts.* With the consent of all the members, the following member or members _____ (list name[s] here) is designated to establish savings, checking, and other such accounts as are necessary for the operation of the business. The same designated member or members shall deposit and withdraw funds from these accounts. The funds of the LLC shall not be commingled with the personal funds of any members of the LLC.

(5) *Tax Returns.* Within 60 days after the end of the tax year of the LLC, a Form K-1 (Partner's Share of Income, Credits, Deductions) and other information as may be necessary for the preparation of each member's federal and state income tax returns, including a statement showing each member's share of income, gain or loss, and credits for the prior tax year of the LLC, shall be provided to each member of the LLC.

Article IV
Capital Structure

(1) *Initial Contributions.* The members initially shall contribute to this LLC the following cash, property, and services, as shown next to each member's name hereafter. A promise by a member to contribute to the LLC is not enforceable unless set out in a writing signed by the member. The initial contributions to the LLC shall be made by _____ (date). The total agreed upon value of all such cash, property, and services is $_____. For each member, the contributions record shown below shall state the value and nature of the contribution and the percentage of membership interest in the LLC, calculated according to the instructions in section II(10) of this Operating Agreement. The fair market value of items of property or services shall be agreed upon between the LLC and the contributing member.

Name of Contributor	Contribution	Fair Market Value	Percentage of Membership Interest in LLC
_____	_____	_____	_____
_____	_____	_____	_____
_____	_____	_____	_____
_____	_____	_____	_____
_____	_____	_____	_____

(2) *Additional Contributions.* (a) The LLC has no right to require any member to make additional contributions, after the initial contribution, except as provided in section (b) below. If the LLC accepted the promise of the performance of future services or the delivery of property at some future date from any member in exchange for a membership interest, this section does not release the member from the obligation to perform those agreed on services or deliver those agreed on properties.

(b) The members may agree, by unanimous vote, to require the members to make additional capital contributions to the LLC by an agreed on date.

(3) *Contributions Legally Obligated.* A member is obligated to the limited liability company to perform any enforceable promise to contribute cash or property or to perform services, even if he or she is unable to perform because of death, disability, or other reason. If a member does not make the required contribution of property or services, he or she is obligated, at the option of the LLC, to contribute cash equal to that portion of value of the stated contribution that has not been made.

The obligation of a member to make a contribution or return money or other property paid or distributed in violation of the Michigan LLC Act may be relaxed or set aside only with the unanimous consent of the members. Notwithstanding the relaxation or setting aside of the obligation, a creditor of an LLC who extends credit or otherwise acts in reliance on that obligation after the member signs a writing that reflects the obligation and before the amendment of the writing to reflect the relaxation or setting aside of the obligation may enforce the original obligation.

If a member is delinquent in his or her promised contributions, the remaining members may also, by unanimous vote, agree to cancel the membership of the delinquent member. Any previous partial payments of the total amount due the LLC are to be refunded promptly, following the decision to cancel the membership of the delinquent member.

(4) *Future Contributions.* A contribution consisting of an obligation to contribute cash or property or services to be performed (such as a promissory note) will be in exchange for a future membership interest, to take effect at the time of the payment of cash, the surrender of property, or the completion of work promised. A future membership interest contingent upon a future contribution of cash or property or services will include a future profits interest, based on the formula for allocating profits and losses discussed below.

(5) *Title to Assets.* All personal and real property of this LLC, including bank accounts, real estate, and equipment, shall be held in the name of the LLC, not the name of individual members.

(6) *Capital Accounts.* The LLC will establish and maintain a capital account for each member on the books of this company. The capital account shall show each member's respective capital contributions to the LLC, with increases for each member's share of profits and decreases for each member's share of expenses of the LLC and losses. The capital account of each member shall be adjusted on a regular basis in accordance with the applicable regulations of the Internal Revenue Code.

(7) *Allocation of Profits and Losses.* (a) No member shall receive preferential treatment in obtaining distributions or allocations of the profits, losses, deductions, or credits of the LLC, with the exceptions noted in section (b) below. For accounting and tax purposes, the LLC's net profits or net losses shall be calculated on an annual basis. This LLC shall allocate profits and losses and all related items of income or loss to each individual member in accordance with each member's percentage ownership in the LLC, with the exceptions noted in section (b).

(b) On account of loans made to the LLC or in the case of other special efforts, such as an innovative idea for a new product or service, a phenomenal sales record, and so on, the LLC, by unanimous vote of the members, may increase, temporarily or permanently, a member's right to share in profits and distributions over and above his or her percentage of financial interest in the company.

(8) *Distributions.* By a majority vote of the members, the LLC may make cash distributions from time to time to its members. Such distributions shall be made in accordance with each member's percentage of interest in the LLC, with the exceptions noted in section IV(7)(b) of this Operating Agreement. All such distributions must be made in light of §450.4307 of the Michigan LLC Act, which states: "A distribution shall not be made if, after giving it effect, the limited liability company would not be able to pay its debts as they become due in the usual course of business or the limited liability company's total assets would be less than the sum of its total liabilities. . . ." A distribution cannot be paid, in other words, if its payment would render the LLC insolvent. The LLC may base its determination that a distribution is not prohibited under this section on financial statements or other accepted and reasonable methods of valuation. Under §450.4308 of the Michigan LLC Act, members who vote for or assent to a distribution in violation of section 307 are personally liable, jointly and severally, to the LLC for the amount of the distribution that exceeds what could have been distributed without violating section 307.

(9) *Termination of LLC.* Upon liquidation of the LLC, after the company has satisfied all its debts and obligations, any remaining assets of the company will be distributed in cash to the members whose interests have not previously been redeemed. First, each member's capital account must be brought up to date, reflecting all credits and deductions. If the company upon liquidation lacks sufficient assets to redeem the amount shown in each member's capital account, the company will make distributions in proportion to the amount in the respective capital accounts of the members. Any assets remaining after satisfying the positive balance in each member's capital account will be divided in accordance with each member's percentage interest in the LLC.

Article V
Records

The LLC shall keep at its registered office all of the following:
(a) A current list of the full name and last known address of each member
(b) A copy of the Articles of Organization, together with any amendments to the articles
(c) Copies of the LLC's federal, state, and local tax returns and reports, if any, for the 3 most recent years

(d) Copies of any financial statements of the LLC for the 3 most recent years
(e) A signed copy of this Operating Agreement
(f) Copies of records that would enable a member to determine the members' relative shares of the LLC's distributions and their relative voting rights

Concerning (d), the LLC shall maintain at its registered office complete and accurate accounting records of the company's business affairs. Such records shall be kept by such method of accounting as specified by the members in Article III(3) of this Operating Agreement. The company's accounting period shall be the calendar year, unless the members agree to a different tax year, as specified in Article III(2) of this Operating Agreement.

Article VI
Membership Withdrawal, Transfer, and Assignment

(1) *Withdrawal.* A member may withdraw from the LLC by giving written notice to all other members at least 90 days before the effective withdrawal date, unless the withdrawal violates the terms of the Operating Agreement. If the withdrawal does violate the terms of the Operating Agreement, the withdrawing member is not entitled to distributions that would otherwise be due, as discussed below. The company may also recover from the withdrawing member in violation of the terms of the Operating Agreement damages for breach of duty (Michigan LLC Act, §450.4509).

A withdrawing member not in violation of the terms of the Operating Agreement is entitled to receive any distribution to which the member is entitled under the Operating Agreement. A withdrawing member is also entitled to receive as a distribution, within a reasonable time after withdrawal, the fair market value of his or her interest in the limited liability company as of the date of withdrawal, based upon the member's right to share in distributions from the LLC.

(2) *Transfer.* A member may not transfer his or her membership in the LLC without unanimous approval of the other members.

(3) *Assignment.* A membership interest in the LLC is assignable in whole or in part. The assignment of membership interest is an assignment of financial interest only. It entitles the assignee to participate in distributions and credits from the LLC. It does not entitle the assignee to any management role in the company. An assignee of a membership interest in the LLC may become a member with management rights only with the unanimous consent of the other members.

Article VII
Mergers and Dissolutions

(1) *Mergers.* A Michigan limited liability company may merge with another limited liability company or any other business entity, as provided in the Michigan LLC Act (§§ 450.4701-450.4706).
(2) *Dissolutions.* A limited liability company is dissolved and its affairs shall be wound up, following the provisions of the Michigan LLC Act (450.4801-450.4808), upon the occurrence of any of the following:
> (a) the expiration of the term of existence specified in the Articles of Organization or this Operating Agreement
> (b) the happening of events specified in the Articles of Organization or this Operating Agreement that are designed to trigger dissolution
> (c) the unanimous consent of all the members
> (d) the entry of a decree of judicial dissolution of the limited liability company under state law
> (e) the death, withdrawal, expulsion, bankruptcy, or dissolution of a member, or the occurrence of any other event that terminates the continued membership of a member of the limited liability company, unless either of the following applies:
>> (i) Within 90 days after the termination of the membership, a majority of the remaining members vote to continue the business of the limited liability and to admit 1 or more members as necessary.
>> (ii) Management of the limited liability company has not been delegated to managers, the Operating Agreement does not allow an assignee to become a member other than by unanimous consent of the other members, and the business of the company is continued as provided in the Operating Agreement (this Operating Agreement provides that the business of the limited liability company is to continue in spite of the termination of a membership).

Article VIII
Management of LLC

(1) *Authority to Bind the Company.* The members acting as a group have sole authority to manage the LLC and to bind the company, making contracts and entering into transactions and making other commitments necessary to conduct the business affairs of this LLC.

        The members as a whole may delegate to any individual member or to any employee of the LLC any particular management responsibility.

(2) *Officers.* The company may designate one or more officers. Many companies choose to designate a Chief Executive Officer and a Chief Financial Officer. If you so choose, fill in the following: The company will retain _____ as Chief Executive Officer of the company and _____ as Chief Financial Officer of the company. Persons who fill these positions may, but need not be, members of the LLC. Such positions may be paid or unpaid, depending on the nature and extent of the duties involved.

Article IX
General Provisions

(1) *Michigan Law Governs.* This Operating Agreement and any questions or disputes arising from it will be governed by the laws of the state of Michigan.

(2) *Severability.* If any provision of this Operating Agreement is determined to be illegal, invalid, or unenforceable, that provision shall be severed from the rest of this Operating Agreement, and the remaining provisions will remain in full force and enforceable.

SIGNATURES OF MEMBERS

Signature: _____

Printed Name: _____, Member

Date: _____

Signature: _____

Printed Name: _____, Member

Date: _____

Signature: _____

Printed Name: _____, Member

Date: _____

Signature: _____

Printed Name: _____, Member

Date: _____

Signature: _____

Printed Name: _____, Member

Date_____

APPENDIX C

Minutes of First Meeting of Members

MINUTES OF FIRST MEETING OF MEMBERS OF
_____

The Members of _____ held its organizational meeting on
_____, 19 _____ at _____ A.M./P.M. at _____
in _____, Michigan.

The following Members were present at the meeting:

_____

_____

_____

_____

_____ was nominated and by unanimous vote elected temporary chairman, and presided over the meeting until relieved by the president.
_____ was nominated and elected by unanimous vote as temporary secretary, and acted as such until relieved by the permanent secretary.

The chairman then presented to the meeting the original copy of the Articles of Organization which had been filed with the Michigan Department of Commerce on _____, 19 _____. The secretary was instructed to append the copy to the minutes of the meeting.

The chairman thereupon presented to the meeting a copy of the proposed Operating Agreement of the limited liability company and read it point by point. After consideration and discussion of each point, it was unanimously resolved that the limited liability company adopt as the Operating Agreement of this limited liability company the Operating Agreement presented to this meeting.

The chairman then presented to the meeting the Preorganization Subscription Agreement (if applicable). As it was read, the contributions to which each Member committed were turned over or signed over to the limited liability company. In the case of the promise of future contributions, these were also read and acknowledged by all the Members.

The following persons were nominated and unanimously elected officers of the limited liability company to serve for one year and until their successors are elected and qualified:
_____ President (Chief Executive Officer)
_____ Secretary
_____ Treasurer (Chief Financial Officer)

The president thereafter presided at the meeting and the permanent secretary replaced the temporary secretary.

Upon motion duly made, seconded, and carried, it was

RESOLVED, that the form of the limited liability company seal presented at the meeting, an impression of which is directed to be made by the secretary in the margin of these minutes, be and hereby is adopted as the seal of this limited liability company.

Upon motion duly made, seconded, and carried, it was further

RESOLVED, that the form of membership certificate submitted to this meeting be and hereby is adopted for the issuance of unit certificates by the president and secretary. A copy of the membership certificate so adopted is to be attached to these minutes, and further

RESOLVED, that the principal executive office of this limited liability company shall be at
_____ in _____, Michigan.

Upon motion duly made, seconded, and carried, it was

RESOLVED, that the fiscal year of this limited liability company shall end on the _____ day of the month of _____ of each year.

Upon motion duly made, seconded, and carried, it was

RESOLVED, that the business will follow the _____ method of accounting.

Upon motion duly made, seconded, and carried, it was:

RESOLVED, that the treasurer be and hereby is authorized to open a bank account with
_____ located at _____ and a resolution for that purpose on the printed form of said bank(s) was adopted and instructed to be attached to these minutes.

Upon motion duly made, seconded, and carried, it was

RESOLVED, that the Medical Reimbursement Plan (if applicable) presented to this meeting be and hereby is adopted as the medical reimbursement plan of the limited liability company.

Upon motion duly made, seconded, and carried, it was

RESOLVED, that the following annual salaries be paid to the officers of this limited liability company.

PRESIDENT; (Chief Executive Officer)
SECRETARY:
TREASURER (Chief Financial Officer):

Upon motion duly made, seconded, and carried, it was

RESOLVED, that whereas the Articles of Organization authorize the limited liability company to issue units of membership interest, this limited liability company shall sell an aggregate of _____ units at a purchase price of $_____ per unit, in consideration of money paid to the limited liability company, as follows:

Name(s) of Purchaser(s)	Number of Units	Amount of Money

RESOLVED FURTHER, that this limited liability company issue an aggregate of _____ units at a purchase price of $_____ per unit, upon delivery of said assets to the limited liability company, as follows:

Name(s) of Purchaser(s)	Number of Units	Description of Property

RESOLVED FURTHER, that this limited liability company issue an aggregative of _____ units of membership interest at a purchase price of $_____ per unit, upon performance of the following services to the limited liability company:

Name(s) of Purchaser(s)	Number of Units	Description of Services

Upon motion duly made, seconded, and carried, it was

RESOLVED, that the limited liability company accept the written offer dated _____, 19 _____,to transfer the assets and liabilities of said business, in accordance with the terms of said offer, a copy of which is attached to the minutes of this meeting.

RESOLVED FURTHER, that all the Members hereby determine that the fair market value of said business to the limited liability company is $_____.

Since there was no further business to come before the meeting, on motion duly made, seconded, and carried, the meeting was adjourned.

DATED:

_____
Secretary

The following are appended hereto:
CERTIFIED COPY OF ARTICLES OF ORGANIZATION
SAMPLE MEMBERSHIP CERTIFICATE
BANK DEPOSITORY RESOLUTION FORM
MEDICAL REIMBURSEMENT PLAN (if applicable)
OFFER OF TRANSFER OF BUSINESS (if applicable)

APPENDIX D

Articles of Organization for Michigan Domestic Professional Service Limited Liability Companies (Form 701)

C&S 701 (Rev. 5/93)

MICHIGAN DEPARTMENT OF COMMERCE - CORPORATION AND SECURITIES BUREAU

Date Received		(FOR BUREAU USE ONLY)

Name	
Address	
City	State	Zip Code

✌ **Document will be returned to the name and address you enter above** ☞

EFFECTIVE DATE: _____

L	C	—			

ARTICLES OF ORGANIZATION
For use by Domestic Professional Service Limited Liability Companies
(Please read information and instructions on last page)

Pursuant to the provisions of Act 23, Public Acts of 1993, the undersigned execute the following Articles:

ARTICLE I

The name of the professional limited liability company is:

ARTICLE II

The limited liability company is organized for the sole and specific purpose of rendering the following professional service(s):

ARTICLE III

The duration of the limited liability company is: _____

ARTICLE IV

1. The address of the registered office is:

   _____ , Michigan _____
   (Street Address)   (City)   (ZIP Code)

2. The mailing address of the registered office if different than above:

   _____ , Michigan _____
   (P.O. Box)   (City)   (ZIP Code)

3. The name of the resident agent at the registered office is: _____

ARTICLE V

All members will be duly licensed or otherwise legally authorized to render one or more of the professional service(s) for which this limited liability company is organized except as otherwise provided in Section 904(2) of this Act or prohibited by law.

Signed this _____ day of _____, 19_____

_____   _____
(Signature)   (Signature)

_____   _____
(Type or Print Name)   (Type or Print Name)

_____   _____
(Signature)   (Signature)

_____   _____
(Type or Print Name)   (Type or Print Name)

Name of Person or Organization
Remitting Fees:

_____

_____

Preparer's Name and Business
Telephone Number:

_____

(   ) _____

INFORMATION AND INSTRUCTIONS

1. The articles of organization cannot be filed until this form, or a comparable document, is submitted.

2. Submit one original of this document. Upon filing, the document will be added to the records of the Corporation and Securities Bureau. The original will be returned to the address you enter in the box on the front as evidence of filing.

   Since this document will be maintained on optical disc media, it is important that the filing be legible. Documents with poor black and white contrast, or otherwise illegible, will be rejected.

3. This document is to be used pursuant to the provisions of Act 23, P.A. of 1993. by two or more persons for the purpose of forming a domestic professional service limited liability company.

4. Article I - The name shall contain the words "Professional Limited Liability Company" or the abbreviation "P.L.L.C." or "P.L.C."

5. Article II - State the specific professional service(s) for which the limited liability company is organized.

6. Article III - The term of existence of the professional limited liability company must be stated.

7. Article IV - A post office box may not be designated as the address of the registered office.

8. Article V - Members must be licensed to perform at least one of the service(s) for which the limited liability company is organized unless otherwise prohibited by law.

   If the professional limited liability company renders a professional service that is included within the public health code, Act No. 368 of the Public Acts of 1978, being sections 333.1101 to 333.25211 of the Michigan Compiled Laws, then all members of the limited liability company shall be licensed or legally authorized in this state to render the same professional service.

9. This document is effective on the date endorsed "Filed" by the Bureau. A later effective date, no more than 90 days after the date of delivery, may be stated as an additional article.

10. The articles must be signed in ink by the organizing members. Names of persons signing shall be stated beneath their signatures.

11. FEES: Make remittance payable to the State of Michigan. Include limited liability company name on check or money order.
    Nonrefundable filing fee **$50.00**

12. Mail form and fee to: The office is located at:

   Michigan Department of Commerce   6546 Mercantile Way
   Corporation and Securities Bureau   Lansing, MI 48910
   Corporation Division   (517) 334-6302
   P.O. Box 30054
   Lansing, MI 48909-7554

APPENDIX E

Application for Reservation of Name
Preorganization Subscription Agreement
Certificate of Formation (Delaware)
Application for Foreign LLCs (Michigan)
Bill of Sale Agreement
Medical and Dental Reimbursement Plan

MICHIGAN DEPARTMENT OF COMMERCE - CORPORATION AND SECURITIES BUREAU		

Date Received:	Date Received:	Extended To:	(FOR BUREAU USE ONLY)
Date Received:	Date Received:	Extended To:	

Name
Address
City   State   Zip Code

EXPIRATION DATE:

↳ **Document will be returned to the name and address you enter above** ↴

APPLICATION FOR RESERVATION OF NAME

For use by Corporations, Limited Partnerships, and Limited Liability Companies

(Please read information and instructions on reverse side)

Pursuant to the provisions of Act 284, Public Acts of 1972 (profit corporations), Act 162, Public Acts of 1982 (nonprofit corporations), Act 213, Public Acts of 1982 (limited partnerships), or Act 23, Public Acts of 1993 (limited liability companies), the undersigned applicant executes the following Application:

1. The name to be reserved is:

2. This name is reserved for use as the name of a (check appropriate box):

   ☐ Profit Corporation (for six months following the month of filing) - $10.00

   ☐ Nonprofit Corporation (for four months following the month of filing) - $10.00

   ☐ Limited Partnership (for four months following the month of filing) - $10.00

   ☐ Limited Liability Company (for six months following the month of filing) - $25.00

Signed this _____ day of _____, 19 _____

_____
(Signature of Applicant)

_____
(Type or Print Name)   (Type or Print Title)

_____
(Street Address)

_____
(City, State, ZIP Code)

The exclusive right to use a name may be transferred to another person. To request a transfer, complete the following:

NOTICE OF TRANSFER OF NAME RESERVATION

Pursuant to Section 215(3), Act 284, Public Acts of 1972; Section 215(3), Act 162, Public Acts of 1982; Section 103(b), Act 213, Public Acts of 1982; or Section 205(2), Act 23, Public Acts of 1993, the undersigned hereby transfers to

_____

_____
(Name and Address of Transferee)

the right to exclusive use of the name _____

_____

_____
(Name of Original Applicant)

By _____
(Signature)

INFORMATION AND INSTRUCTIONS

1. Submit one original of this document. Upon filing, the document will be added to the records of the Corporation and Securities Bureau. The original will be returned to the address in the box on the front as evidence of filing.

    Since this document will be maintained on optical disk media, it is important that the filing be legible. Documents with poor black and white contrast, or otherwise illegible, will be rejected.

2. If the name is available, the administrator shall reserve it for exclusive use of the applicant.

    Nonprofit Corporations or Limited Partnerships: The Administrator, for good cause shown, may extend the reservation for periods of not more than two calendar months each. No more than two extensions shall be granted. Extension requests must be received in writing by the Bureau prior to the expiration of the reservation period.

    Profit Corporations and Limited Liability Companies: Upon expiration, the name may again be reserved by filing another application and fee.

3. Act 284, Public Acts of 1972; Act 192, Public Acts of 1962; Act 213, Public Acts of 1982; and Act 23, Public Acts of 1993 require certain words or abbreviations be included or excluded from the name of profit corporations, limited partnerships, or limited liability companies. Those required are:
    a. Company, Corporation, Incorporated, Limited, Co., Corp., Inc., or Ltd. in the name of domestic (non-professional service) corporations.
    b. Professional Corporation or P.C. in the name of professional service corporations.
    c. Limited Partnership in the name of limited partnerships.
    d. Limited Liability Company, L.L.C., or L.C. in the name of (non-professional service) limited liability companies.
    e. Professional Limited Liability Company, P.L.L.C., or P.L.C. in the name of professional service limited liability companies.

    Those excluded are: Corporation, Incorporated, Corp., Inc. in the name of limited partnerships and limited liability companies.

4. The application for reservation of name and the notice of transfer of name reservation must be signed in ink by the applicant.

5. FEES: Make remittance payable to the State of Michigan. No fee for transfer or extension of reservation. **Nonrefundable filing fee**
    CORPORATION OR LIMITED PARTNERSHIP $10.00
    LIMITED LIABILITY COMPANY $25.00

6. Mail form and fee to:
    Michigan Department of Commerce
    Corporation and Securities Bureau
    Corporation Division
    P.O. Box 30054
    Lansing, MI 48909-7554

    The Office is located at:
    6546 Mercantile Way
    Lansing, MI 48910
    Telephone (517) 334-6302

PREORGANIZATION SUBSCRIPTION AGREEMENT

We, the undersigned, severally subscribe to the number of units set opposite our respective names of capital of a proposed limited liability company, to be known as _____ or by any other name that the members may select, and to be organized in the State of Michigan. We agree to pay the sum of $_____ per each unit subscribed.

This subscription shall not be binding on the undersigned unless subscriptions in the aggregate amount of $_____ for units of said limited liability company have been procured on or before the _____ day of _____, 19 _____.

All subscriptions hereto shall be payable at such time or times as the members of said limited liability company may determine and shall be paid in cash, except as hereinafter indicated. (If any of the subscriptions are to be paid by transferring property or offering services to the limited liability company, a description of the property and/or services shall be attached hereto.)

Date	Name and Address	Number of Units	Amount Subscribed

STATE *of* DELAWARE
LIMITED LIABILITY COMPANY
CERTIFICATE *of* FORMATION

▶ **FIRST:** The name of the limited liability company is _____

_____

▶ **SECOND:** The address of its registered office in the State of Delaware is _____

_____ in the City of _____ , County

of _____ . The name of its Registered Agent at such address is

_____

_____

▶ **THIRD:** (Use this paragraph only if the company is to have a specific effective date of dissolution:

"The latest date on which the limited liability company is to dissolve is _____ .")

▶ **FOURTH:** (Insert any other matters the members determine to include herein.)

_____

_____

_____

_____

_____

_____

▶ **IN WITNESS WHEREOF,** the undersigned have executed this Certificate of Formation of

_____ this day of _____ , 19 _____ .

_____
Authorized Person(s)

_____

_____

C&S-760 (Rev 5/94)

<table>
<tr><td colspan="3">MICHIGAN DEPARTMENT OF COMMERCE - CORPORATION AND SECURITIES BUREAU</td></tr>
<tr><td>Date Received:</td><td></td><td rowspan="2">(FOR BUREAU USE ONLY)</td></tr>
<tr><td></td><td></td></tr>
</table>

Name

Address

City   State   Zip Code

☜ Document will be returned to the name and address you enter above ☞

EFFECTIVE DATE:

| L | C | — | | | |

APPLICATION FOR CERTIFICATE OF AUTHORITY
TO TRANSACT BUSINESS IN MICHIGAN
For use by Foreign Limited Liability Companies
(Please read information and instructions on last page)

Pursuant to the provisions of Act 23, Public Acts of 1993, the undersigned limited liability company executes the following Application:

1. The name of the limited liability company is:

   _____

2. (Complete this item only if the limited liability company name in item 1 is not available for use in Michigan.) The assumed name of the limited liability company to be used in all its dealings with the Bureau and in the transaction of its business in Michigan is:

   _____

3. It is organized under the laws of _____.

   The date of its organization is _____.

   The duration of its existence is until _____.

4. The address of the office required to be maintained in the state of organization or, if not so required, the principal office of the limited liability company is:

   _____
   (Street Address)   (City)   (State)   (ZIP Code)

5. a. The address of its registered office in Michigan is:

_____ , Michigan _____
(Street Address)   (City)   (ZIP Code)

b. The mailing address of the registered office if different than above:

_____ , Michigan _____
(P.O. Box)   (City)   (ZIP Code)

c. The name of the resident agent at the registered office is:

_____

6. The Department is appointed the agent of the foreign limited liability company for service of process if no agent has been appointed, or if appointed, the agent's authority has been revoked, the agent has resigned, or the agent cannot be found or served through the exercise of reasonable diligence.

The name and address of a member or manager or other person to whom the administrator is to send copies of any process served on the administrator is:

_____
(Name)

_____
(Street Address)   (City)   (State)   (ZIP Code)

7. The specific business which the limited liability company is to transact in Michigan is as follows:

The limited liability company is authorized to transact such business in the jurisdiction of its organization.

Signed this _____ day of _____ , 19 _____

By _____
                         (Signature)

_____
(Type or Print Name)   (Type or Print Title)

INFORMATION AND INSTRUCTIONS

1. The application for certificate of authority to transact business cannot be filed until this form, or a comparable document, is submitted.

2. Submit one original of this document. Upon filing, the document will be added to the records of the Corporation and Securities Bureau. The original will be returned to the address you enter in the box on the front accompanied by a certificate of authority.

   Since this document will be maintained on optical disc media, it is important that the filing be legible. Documents with poor black and white contrast, or otherwise illegible, will be rejected.

3. This document is to be used pursuant to the provisions of Article 10 of the Act by a foreign limited liability company for the purpose of obtaining a certificate of authority to transact business in this state. If the foreign limited liability company subsequently changes any of the information set forth in the Application for Certificate of Authority, it must file an Amended Application for Certificate of Authority to Transact Business in Michigan (form C&S 762) with the Bureau not later than 30 days after the time a change becomes effective.

4. Item 2 - A foreign limited liability company whose true name is not available for use in Michigan is permitted to apply for a Certificate of Authority under an assumed name which is available for use. The assumed name becomes the limited liability company's name in Michigan to be used in all transactions and in its dealings with the administrator. Item 2 of the Application for Certificate of Authority to Transact Business in Michigan is to be completed for this purpose only. Limited liability companies may also transact business under other assumed names by filing separate Certificates of Assumed Name.

5. Item 7 - This item should state only the specific business to be transacted in Michigan. An all purpose activities statement is not permitted.

6. The application must be signed in ink by a person with authority to sign as provided in the laws of the jurisdiction of its organization.

7. Attach to this application a certificate stating that the limited liability company is in good standing under the laws of the jurisdiction of its organization; dated no earlier than 30 days prior to the date of receipt in this office. The certificate must be executed by the official of the jurisdication having custody of limited liability company records.

8. This document is effective on the date endorsed "Filed" by the Bureau. A later effective date, no more than 90 days after the date of delivery, may be stated.

9. FEES: Make remittance payable to the State of Michigan. Include limited liability company name and identification number on check or money order. **Nonrefundable filing fee** **$50.00**

10. Mail form and fee to:

    Michigan Department of Commerce
    Corporation and Securities Bureau
    Corporation Division
    P.O. Box 30054
    Lansing, MI 48909-7554

    The Office is located at:

    6546 Mercantile Way
    Lansing, MI 48910
    (517) 334-6302

BILL OF SALE AGREEMENT

The limited liability company, _____, and the business owner(s) _____, hereafter called the "transferor(s)," enter into the following agreement:

       1. In return for the issuance and delivery of _____ membership units of _____ _____, a Michigan limited liability company, I (we) hereby sell, assign, and transfer to the limited liability company all my (our) right, title, and interest in the following property:

       a. All the tangible assets listed on the inventory attached to this Bill of Sale, and all stock in trade, trade, goodwill, trade names, trademarks, service marks, leasehold interests, copyrights and other intangible assets (excluding—list any non-transferred assets: _____) of _____, located at _____ Street, _____, _____ County, Michigan.

       2. In return for the transfer of the above property to it, the limited liability company hereby agrees to assume, pay, and discharge all debts, duties, and obligations that appear on the date of this agreement, on the books and owed on account of said business (excluding—list any unassumed liabilities:). The limited liability company agrees to indemnify and hold the transferor(s) of said business and their property free from any liability for any such debt, duty, or obligation and from any suits, actions, or legal proceedings brought to enforce or collect any such debt, duty, or obligation.

       3. The transferor(s) hereby appoint(s) the limited liability company as his (her, their) representative to demand, receive, and collect for itself, all debts and obligations now owing to said business (excluding—list any unassumed debts:). The transferor(s) further authorize(s) the limited liability company to do all things allowed by law to recover and collect such debts and obligations and to use the transferor's (s') name(s) in such manner as it considers necessary for the collection and recovery of such debts and obligations, provided, however, without cost, expense, or damage to the transferor(s).

DATED:

_____
(Transferor)

_____
(Transferor)

_____
(Transferor)

_____
(Name of Limited Liability Company)
By: _____
           (Title)

_____
           (Title)

MEDICAL AND DENTAL CARE REIMBURSEMENT PLAN
OF

_____

1. BENEFITS

The limited liability company shall reimburse all eligible employees for expenses incurred by themselves and their dependents, as defined in IRC S152, as amended, for medical care, as defined in IRC S213(e), as amended, subject to the conditions and limitations as hereinafter set forth. Any benefits payable to eligible employees under this Plan will be included in their gross income and subject to tax.

2. ELIGIBILITY

All company officers and employees employed on a full-time basis at the date of inception of this Plan, including those who may be absent due to illness or injury on said date, are eligible employees under the Plan. A company officer or employee shall be considered employed on a full-time basis if said officer or employee customarily works at least seven months in each year and twenty hours in each week. Any person hereafter becoming an officer or employee of the company, employed on a full-time basis, shall be eligible under this Plan.

3. LIMITATIONS

(a) The company shall reimburse any eligible employee without limitation/no more than $_____ (cross out one) in any fiscal year for medical care expenses.

(b) Reimbursement or payment provided under this Plan shall be made by the company only in the event and to the extent that such reimbursement or payment is not provided under any insurance policy(ies), whether owned by the company or the employee, or under any other health and accident or wage continuation plan. In the event that there is such an insurance policy or plan in effect, providing for reimbursement in whole or in part, then to the extent of the coverage under such policy or plan, the company shall be relieved of any and all liability hereunder.

4. SUBMISSION OF PROOF

Any eligible employee applying for reimbursement under this Plan shall submit to the company, at least quarterly, all bills for medical care, including premium notices for accident or health insurance, for verification by the company prior to payment. Failure to comply herewith may, at the discretion of the company, terminate such eligible employee's rights to said reimbursement.

5. DISCONTINUATION

This Plan shall be subject to termination at any time by vote of the members of the limited liability company; provided, however, that medical care expenses incurred prior to such termination shall be reimbursed or paid in accordance with the terms of this Plan.

6. DETERMINATION

The chief executive officer shall determine all questions arising from the administration and interpretation of the Plan except where reimbursement is claimed by the chief executive officer. In such case, determination shall be made by the members.

APPENDIX F

Membership Certificates

Certificate Number _____

_____ Units _____

A LIMITED LIABILITY COMPANY ORGANIZED UNDER THE LAWS OF THE STATE OF MICHIGAN

This Certifies That _____ is a member of the above named Limited Liability Company and is the owner of _____ Units of the said company. He/she is entitled to the full rights and privileges of such membership, subject to the restrictions in the Articles of Organization and Operating Agreement for the Limited Liability Company.

The membership interest represented by this Certificate is subject to restrictions on transfer, a copy of which is available free of charge upon request from an officer of the LLC at the following address:

_____

In Witness Whereof, the said Limited Liability Company has caused this Certificate to be signed by its duly authorized Member(s)/Manager(s) and to be sealed with the seal of the Limited Liability Company.

Date _____

Certificate Number _____

Units _____

A LIMITED LIABILITY COMPANY ORGANIZED UNDER THE LAWS OF THE STATE OF MICHIGAN

This Certifies That

above named Limited Liability Company and is the owner of _____ is a member of the company. He/she is entitled to the full rights and privileges of such membership, subject to the restrictions in the Articles of Organization and Operating Agreement for the Limited Liability Company.

The membership interest represented by this Certificate is subject to restrictions on transfer, a copy of which is available free of charge upon request from an officer of the LLC at the following address:

_____

In Witness Whereof, the said Limited Liability Company has caused this Certificate to be signed by its duly authorized Member(s)/Manager(s) and to be sealed with the seal of the Limited Liability Company.

Date _____

_____

Certificate Number _____

Units _____

A LIMITED LIABILITY COMPANY ORGANIZED UNDER THE LAWS OF THE STATE OF MICHIGAN

This Certifies That

above named Limited Liability Company and is the owner of _____ is a member of the _____ Units of the said company. He/she is entitled to the full rights and privileges of such membership, subject to the restrictions in the Articles of Organization and Operating Agreement for the Limited Liability Company.

The membership interest represented by this Certificate is subject to restrictions on transfer, a copy of which is available free of charge upon request from an officer of the LLC at the following address:

In Witness Whereof, the said Limited Liability Company has caused this Certificate to be signed by its duly authorized Member(s)/Manager(s) and to be sealed with the seal of the Limited Liability Company.

Date _____

Certificate Number _____

Units _____

A LIMITED LIABILITY COMPANY ORGANIZED UNDER THE LAWS OF THE STATE OF MICHIGAN

This Certifies That

above named Limited Liability Company and is the owner of _____ is a member of the company. He/she is entitled to the full rights and privileges of such membership, subject to the restrictions in the Articles of Organization and Operating Agreement for the Limited Liability Company.

The membership interest represented by this Certificate is subject to restrictions on transfer, a copy of which is available free of charge upon request from an officer of the LLC at the following address: _____

In Witness Whereof, the said Limited Liability Company has caused this Certificate to be signed by its duly authorized Member(s)/Manager(s) and to be sealed with the seal of the Limited Liability Company.

Date _____

Certificate Number _____

Units _____

A LIMITED LIABILITY COMPANY ORGANIZED UNDER THE LAWS OF THE STATE OF MICHIGAN

This Certifies That

above named Limited Liability Company and is the owner of _____ is a member of the company. He/she is entitled to the full rights and privileges of such membership, subject to the restrictions in the Articles of Organization and Operating Agreement for the Limited Liability Company.

The membership interest represented by this Certificate is subject to restrictions on transfer, a copy of which is available free of charge upon request from an officer of the LLC at the following address:

_____

In Witness Whereof, the said Limited Liability Company has caused this Certificate to be signed by its duly authorized Member(s)/Manager(s) and to be sealed with the seal of the Limited Liability Company.

Date _____

Certificate Number _____

Units _____

A LIMITED LIABILITY COMPANY ORGANIZED UNDER THE LAWS OF THE STATE OF MICHIGAN

This Certifies That

above named Limited Liability Company and is the owner of _____ is a member of the company. He/she is entitled to the full rights and privileges of such membership, subject to the restrictions in the Articles of Organization and Operating Agreement for the Limited Liability Company.

The membership interest represented by this Certificate is subject to restrictions on transfer, a copy of which is available free of charge upon request from an officer of the LLC at the following address:

_____

In Witness Whereof, the said Limited Liability Company has caused this Certificate to be signed by its duly authorized Member(s)/Manager(s) and to be sealed with the seal of the Limited Liability Company.

Date _____

Limited Liability Company Checklist

Action	Pages where discussed	Completed
1. Select your LLC name (***Read*** Naming Your Business and Its Products and Services; ***Contact The P. Gaines Co. for trade name and trademark searches***)	*58-61*	
2. Prepare your Articles of Organization	*61-64*	
3. File your Articles of Organization	*64*	
4. Apply for LLC Employer Identification Number	*75-76*	
5. Order the LLC Records Book and Seal	*66*	
6. Prepare the Preorganization Subscription Agreement (if applicable)	*67-69*	
7. Prepare the Operating Agreement	*69*	
8. Prepare the Minutes of the First Meeting	*69-71*	
9. Issue Membership Certificates	*72-75*	
10. File Assumed Name Report (if applicable)	*76*	

IMPORTANT ADDRESSES AND PHONE NUMBERS

MICHIGAN DEPARTMENT OF COMMERCE

Corporation Division
PO Box 30054
Lansing, Michigan 48909
Telephone (517) 334-6206

Securities Division
PO Box 30222
Lansing, Michigan 48909
Telephone (517) 334-6200

New Business Startups
Will answer questions,
provide information packet.
Telephone (517) 373-9808

BUSINESS INFORMATION LINES

Name check for availability
of LLC names

Telephone 1-900-555-0031 (cost of $1.50 per minute—very fast)

Document Review Section
(for assistance with filling out
LLC Articles of Organization)

Telephone (517) 334-6302

Records Information Unit
(photocopies of filed documents)

Telephone 1-900-555-0031 (cost of $1.50 per minute)

DEPARTMENT OF THE TREASURY
430 W. Allegan Street
Lansing, Michigan 48922
Sales Tax (517) 373-3190
Single Business Tax (517) 373-8030

Regarding the hiring of employees, including yourself, contact:
Bureau of Workers Compensation
PO Box 30016
Lansing, Michigan 48909
Telephone (517) 322-1195

Michigan Employment Security Commission
7310 Woodward Avenue
Detroit, Michigan 48202
Telephone 1-800-638-3994; (313) 876-6691; (517) 334-6726

CHARITABLE FOUNDATION SECTION
Office of the Attorney General
525 W Ottawa
Law Building, Room 670
Lansing, Michigan 48913
[Mailing address: PO Box 30214
Lansing, Michigan 48909]
Telephone (517) 373-1152
If you plan to solicit donations, you must register with this office.

INTERNAL REVENUE SERVICE
IRS Taxpayer Assistance: 1-800-829-1040; *to request forms and publications*: 1-800-829-3676

ZONING AND LICENSING
Be sure to contact the county clerk and the city
clerk in the area in which you live in regard
to zoning and any licenses or permits required
to conduct business in their jurisdiction, including
home-based businesses.

Index

M

N

The Black Beauty LLC Outfit

By special arrangement with Julius Blumberg, Inc., The P. Gaines Co. will provide a complete LLC kit with the following outstanding features:

1. A three-ring LLC Record Book with 24K gold trim and lustrous black vinyl slip case. LLC name is printed on a gold label and inserted into acetate label holder. Record Book includes Mylar-coated Index Tabs, with eight important divisions (Articles of Organization, Operating Agreement, Regulations, Members, Unit Certificates, Transfer Ledger, Minutes, and Financial Reports), and 50 blank sheets of rag content 20-lb. bond Minute Paper.

2. An LLC Seal stored inside the LLC Record Book in a zipper pouch, 1 5/8" diameter, custom finished with LLC name, state, and year. Long LLC names (over 45 characters and spaces) require a 2" diameter seal, at an extra charge of $8.00.

3. 20 custom printed and numbered Unit Certificates with full page numbered stubs. Each certificate is custom printed with LLC name, state, and member titles.

ORDER FORM—Remit with payment to The P. Gaines Co., Box 2253, Oak Park, IL 60303

For all LLC kit orders, please type or print the following information:

LLC name exactly as on Articles of Organization...

State of organization..

Year of organization..

Each certificate will provide space for two members to sign, whose titles will be designated as "Managing Members"

Basic price of LLC kit	$69.95
For long LLC names	
(over 45 characters and spaces), add an additional $8.00	_.__
7.75% Illinois sales tax (Illinois residents only)	5.42

Choose **one** of the following two modes of shipping and cross out the other:

Shipping by UPS (delivery within 2 weeks from receipt of your order)	4.00
OR Shipping by Air Express (delivery within 4 days from receipt of order)	25.00

(*4-day Air Express orders must be paid for with Certified Check, Money Order, or credit card)

TOTAL _____

Ship to:

Your name...Address...Phone................

(Street address required)

City...State...Zip.............................

Charge to my: _____Visa _____Mastercard

Card#:_____Expires:_____

Exact name on credit card_____

New from P. Gaines

*Five Easy Steps to Setting Up
an IRS-Approved Retirement Plan
for Your Small Business (Incorporated
or Unincorporated), With Forms*

"Less than 20 percent of small businesses in this country have retirement plans for their employees. As a result, businesses with 25 or fewer employees cover an average of only one in seven workers with company pension plans."

With this premise in mind, a new book by Phillip Williams, *Five Easy Steps to Setting Up an IRS-Approved Retirement Plan for Your Small Business*, begins. The key problem is shown to be a lack of money only *sometimes*. Typically, it is either poor planning or a lack of awareness, due to a complete absence of even the most basic information about the subject. *Five Easy Steps. . .* focuses on the message that almost any business that is profitable enough to pay its employee(s) a salary can now start a pension fund under recently passed federal legislation.

Drolly illustrated and wittily written, *Five Easy Steps. . .* takes a fresh look at the familiar conundrum of Chateau d'Yquem taste on a diet cola budget and today's version of the story of the grasshopper and the ant-with-a-pension-plan. The book shows the advantages of Simplified Employee Pensions (SEPs) for most small businesses, whether self-employed (sole proprietors), partnerships, or corporations, and walks the reader step-by-step through the process of setting up and maintaining an SEP. All needed IRS forms are appended.

Five Easy Steps. . . shows why an SEP allows complete funding flexibility, with a retirement arrangement that may be employer financed, employee financed, or a combination of each. It points out that the percentage of employee salaries to be contributed to a retirement plan may be reset *each* year, up to a maximum of 15 percent of salary per employee per year or $30,000, whichever is less. It fully explains the procedure for integrating an SEP with Social Security. It emphasizes other advantages as well, such as the option (not permitted in certain other types of plans) of making contributions in profitable years or skipping pension set-asides entirely in lean years.

Certain disadvantages of SEPs, which might make Keoghs, 401(k) plans, or defined benefit pension plans more attractive under some circumstances are also covered.

This lively and enlightening guide will do more to awaken the American small business person to the necessity of retirement planning and the concrete way to go about it than twenty dry-as-dust books on the same topic from major trade publishers.

"The first in a series dubbed the Small Business Bookshelf discusses the benefits and variety of IRS-approved retirement programs available to small businesses. . . . A good how-to manual"--American Library Association's *Booklist*.

ISBN 0-936284-33-1   quality paperback, 8 1/2 x 11, $14.95, indexed

Small Business Bookshelf Series
Volume 2 (ISBN 0-936284-10-2)   **$19.95**

NAMING YOUR BUSINESS AND ITS PRODUCTS AND SERVICES:
How To Create Effective Trade Names, Trademarks, and Service Marks To Attract Customers, Protect Your Good Will And Reputation, And Stay Out Of Court

Every business, no matter how small, needs a company trade name. In addition, manufacturers and companies providing services to the public may require distinctive names for their goods (trademarks) and services (service marks). This book explains the crucial differences between these three types of names used in commerce, the name selection process, and the legal cautions and pitfalls.

Topics covered include:
• The difference between trademarks, copyrights, and patents
• What determines ownership of a trademark or service mark
• Why trade names are *not* registrable with the Patent and Trademark Office (PTO)
• Why *all* trade names, whether used by sole proprietors, partnerships, or corporations, should be "cleared" for possible infringements of other trade names, trademarks, and service marks
• Why existing businesses that failed to research their trade names for possible legal violations before going into business should do so *now*, instead of later
• Why clearance of a name by the Corporation Division of a given state offers no guarantee of trademark or trade name clearance
• How to do computer and manual trademark and trade name searches, including the use of the TRADEMARKSCAN® data base, Shepard's *Citations,* and industry and trade directories
• How what you don't know *can* hurt you in the realm of trademark law
• The main differences between state and federal trademark laws
• The 8 advantages of federal trademark registration
• The federal trademark registration process; the differences between the Principal Register and the Secondary Register
• Why family surnames are disallowed as registrable trademarks or service marks by the PTO, with one exception
• The risks and rewards of names that parody or satirize, such as LARDASHE® jeans for overweight people
• Why you do *not* have to register your trademark or service mark with the PTO in order to use the symbol™
• Why you *must* register your trademark or service mark with the PTO to use the symbol ®
• Why a term that is "merely descriptive" of a company's goods or services, such as "Lite" (for a type of beer) or "Super glue"(for a type of super-adhesive) cannot be registered as a trademark
• The use of symbols, puns, and historical, mythical, and literary allusions as effective marks
• Name-coining techniques

The P. Gaines Co. now offers computer trademark and service mark searches and company name searches. **Both types of seach include:** (1) a computer search of Dun and Bradstreet's Electronic Business Directory, a listing of some 9 million U.S. businesses; (2) a computer search of TRADEMARKSCAN®, scanning both the currently active state and federal trademark registrations in all classes; (3) a computer search of TRADE NAME DATABASE, consisting of trade names and common law trademarks (not registered) as well as registered trademarks compiled by Gale Research in Brands and Their Companies.; (4) a search of some 20 additional data bases where business names appear is also included. Check the order form for additional information.

Order Form

Remit check or M.O. with order to The P. Gaines Co., PO Box 2253, Oak Park, IL 60303

Credit Card Orders: Mail in order (supply information below) or call tollfree: 1-800-578-3853

Title	Cost	Number of copies	Total
How to Form Your Own Michigan LLC* (*Limited Liability Company) Before the Ink Dries!	$26.95		
Small Time Operator	$14.95		
Five Easy Steps to Setting Up a Retirement Plan	$14.95		
The Partnership Book	$26.95		
Starting and Operating a Business in Michigan	$24.95		
Naming Your Business and Its Products & Services	$19.95		
Pennsylvania Incorporation Manual (1st ed)	$24.95		
Illinois Incorporation Manual, With Disk (5th ed)	$31.95		
Michigan Incorporation Manual (2nd ed)	$24.95		
Ohio Incorporation Manual (2nd ed)	$24.95		
Indiana Incorporation Manual, With Disk (2nd ed)	$31.95		
Missouri Incorporation Manual (1st ed)	$19.95		
Minnesota Incorporation Manual (1st ed)	$24.95		
How to Write a Business Plan	$21.95		
Clearing Your Business Name (Computer search)	$95.00		

Check one: ❏ Company Trade Name Search

Name of Company: _____

Main Business Activity: _____

Or   ❏ Trademark or Service Mark Search

Name of product or service: _____

Type of goods or services:_____

Subtotal			
7.75% sales tax (Illinois residents only)			
Shipping ($3.50 for first book; $1.00 for each additional title)			
GRAND TOTAL (please enclose check , M.O., or credit card information)			

Name...

Address...Phone...

Charge to my: _____Visa _____Mastercard
Card#:_____Expires:_____

Exact name on credit card_____

Signature:_____